BETTY CROCKER'S
WEDDING PLAN-BOOK

Illustrations by ELLA GEORGE CALDERON

 GOLDEN PRESS / NEW YORK

Western Publishing Company, Inc.

Racine, Wisconsin

Dear Bride-to-be—

Your wedding day is a day like no other. It is, at once, a very public time and a very private time. It's a time for tradition and a time to express some very personal tastes and feelings and beliefs.

And that's exactly what your wedding should be: a unique blending of the old and the new, the conventional and the individual—an only-one-of-its-kind wedding that is yours and yours alone.

In this book you will get a picture of many of the options open to you. And we urge you to make your choices freely: to take what you want, discard whatever is meaningless to you, and then to add something of your very own.

And to celebrate your wedding—in your own way—you will find a special collection of do-it-yourself menus and recipes for wedding receptions and parties from a brunch for twelve to a buffet for fifty, even a simple afternoon celebration for one hundred and fifty—complete with wedding cakes and decorating ideas. Easy-to-follow directions and serving suggestions provide all the help you need to handle these parties at home.

But there is another side to your wedding too—the purely practical side. Regardless of the kind of wedding you have chosen, it will require organizing. So we have also designed this book as a kind of "central office" for all your wedding business: a place to make notes, file papers, record gifts, check progress—a complete rundown of what's been done and what still needs doing. Really *use* it. Jot notes in it a dozen times a day, take it to the telephone with you, have it by your side as you open presents, tuck papers in it, check things off, cross things out, and perhaps scribble down comments on anything wonderful or funny or even exasperating that happens.

And then perhaps you will keep it to look back on later, as a delightful reminder of everything that went into making your wedding truly yours.

With best wishes,

Betty Crocker

CONTENTS

SO YOU'VE SAID YES

A chat between fiancé and father? A nice idea from long ago. Do what you can to encourage it.

The "right" man has asked you to marry him, and you've said, "Yes." This, then, is the beginning of one of the most exciting—and busiest—times in your life, a time that calls for lots of planning.

SHARING THE NEWS

Tell your parents before you tell anybody else. Share your happy plans with them, alone or with your fiancé present. If you are living in another city, telephone or write. In either case, plan what you're going to say. Make it simple and straightforward, and answer any questions truthfully.

If your family doesn't know your fiancé, arrange a meeting as soon as possible. If you haven't met his parents, try to visit them too. If at all feasible, the two families should get together before the wedding.

Tell very special friends and relatives. Even if you're planning a surprise announcement party, you'll want to let a few people close to you know beforehand.

YOUR ENGAGEMENT RING

Decide whether you want one, and discuss your feelings with your fiancé. Perhaps you'd rather have an amethyst than a diamond. Or maybe you'd like to have a family stone (either family's) reset. You might even prefer to have a bracelet to mark the occasion.

It's a good idea to go together to a reputable jeweler to make your choice. You might possibly want to pick out your wedding band (and your fiancé's too) at the same time.

If your fiancé has surprised you with a ring and you truly don't like the stone or setting, it may be wise to speak up. (Chances are it can be exchanged.) Or grin and wear it. You know best.

YOUR ANNOUNCEMENT

In the papers. See page 26.

At a party. An announcement party, usually given by your parents or a close relative, is completely optional—but it is a festive way of spreading the happy word.

Surprise announcement parties seem to have become a thing of the past, but some of the traditions linger. Your father may lead off the party with a toast to you and your fiancé, and a cake decorated with your names or initials may highlight the occasion. (See the index for appropriate punch and cake recipes.) Remember too that the newspaper announcement should appear the day after the party.

PRESENTS

If someone sends you an engagement present, write a thank-you note immediately and tell them a bit about your wedding plans.

If you want to give your fiancé a gift, choose something personal and permanent: a key ring, cufflinks, a framed photograph of you. Or give him something he particularly wants: a record album, ski boots, or chess set.

YOUR WEDDING YOUR WAY

Maybe the wedding date is just around the corner. Or perhaps you and your fiancé view your engagement as a strictly private affair. Whatever the reason, it's perfectly acceptable to dispense with ring, announcement, or any of the usual conventions. (One exception: Do tell both families.) When the time comes, you simply send out the wedding invitations.

YOUR WEDDING CALENDAR

FIRST OF ALL...
□ **1** Decide what kind of wedding you'd like to have—formal, informal, or somewhere in between. What time of day? What size? What sort of reception? (See page 9.)

□ **2** Do your wishes clash with your budget? The costs of a wedding can run from a few hundred dollars for a simple ceremony and a very small reception to many thousands of dollars for a large gathering with full professional services. Discuss the budget with your parents. Since your father will probably be bearing the bulk of the expenses, he should have a prominent voice in these matters.

□ **3** Select the date and the hour you'd like.

□ **4** Decide where you want to be married. In a church? A club or hotel? Where your parents live or where you are living? Who will officiate? Check at once to make sure both the place and person are available.

□ **5** Make an appointment to talk to the clergyman (see page 10). If you've decided on a civil ceremony, contact a magistrate and make the necessary arrangements.

□ **6** Determine the number of guests you want to attend. Then let your fiancé's mother know what your plans are (see page 18).

□ **7** Decide on the type of reception you want. If it's to be at a club or hotel, make the necessary reservations. Find out exactly what services are included and what options are available. Ask to have firm prices quoted in writing before you confirm. If the reception's to be at home, will you handle it yourself, use a full catering service, or hire a few people to help with the serving?

AND THEN...
□ **1** Choose your attendants (see page 14).

□ **2** Shop for your wedding dress (see page 27).

□ **3** Start on your guest list (see page 18).

□ **4** Find a quality stationer and order invitations, announcements, any enclosure cards, informals, calling cards, and stationery for your thank-you notes (see pages 19-25).

□ **5** Look for a good bridal photographer (see page 28).

□ **6** Shop for the attendants' dresses (see page 14).

□ **7** Help your mother shop for her dress. Keep the groom's mother clued in too so that she can coordinate her costume.

☐ **8** Make a date to see the florist (see page 29).

☐ **9** Start shopping for your trousseau (see page 27).

☐ **10** Choose your silver, china, and crystal patterns; register your preferences at local stores.

☐ **11** Begin addressing invitation and announcement envelopes (see pages 19-20).

Your Personal Notes:

_____

_____

_____

_____

_____

_____

_____

_____

ABOUT ONE MONTH BEFORE THE WEDDING

☐ **1** Mail the invitations.

☐ **2** Arrange for final dress fittings for yourself and your attendants.

☐ **3** Buy lingerie, shoes, and accessories for your gown.

☐ **4** Make an appointment for a physical examination and blood tests. Get a dental checkup, too.

☐ **5** Choose a wedding present for the groom and gifts for your attendants.

☐ **6** Plan the wedding and reception music.

☐ **7** Arrange for wedding-day transportation (see page 30).

☐ **8** Check on lodging for out-of-town guests and relatives.

☐ **9** Coordinate your clothes for the wedding trip.

☐ **10** Plan your gift display if there is to be one (see page 33).

☐ **11** If you are moving to another city, make arrangements so that the wedding gifts will be packed and shipped as soon as you return from your wedding trip.

☐ **12** Keep up with your thank-you notes for wedding gifts.

☐ **13** Finalize food and drink plans for the reception.

☐ **14** Order the wedding cake.

☐ **15** Get your marriage license. Call City Hall or your marriage license bureau to find out what papers you should bring—birth or baptismal certificates, blood-test results—and if you are under age, whether they require the presence of a parent or a written statement of parental consent. Inquire how long a marriage license is valid—usually about a month.

☐ **16** Attend to as many business details as possible:
  a. Get your Social Security card changed to your new name.
  b. Get your driver's license changed.
  c. Discuss with your fiancé how you'll handle bank accounts and charge accounts, jointly or separately.
  d. Have all charge accounts changed, or cancelled if you're moving out of town.
  e. Change the beneficiary designation on any life insurance policies, bonds, or other holdings.
  f. Make a will.
  g. Be sure you are both covered by medical and hospitalization policies.

Note: Not all of these business transactions must or even can be made before the wedding; we include them to remind you that they should be taken care of as soon as possible.

☐ **17** Finish addressing the announcements.

☐ **18** Arrange for the bridesmaids' party and for the rehearsal dinner if your family is giving one.

☐ **19** Plan where you and your attendants will dress on the wedding day. Let them know.

☐ **20** Make last-minute checks on all delivery dates.

☐ **21** Discuss specific shots with the wedding photographer.

☐ **22** Make an appointment to have your hair and nails done a day or so before the wedding. Then why not splurge and ask the hairdresser to come and comb you out the day of the wedding?

☐ **23** Keep the groom's family posted as you finalize your plans. This is very important.

Your Personal Notes:

_____

_____

_____

_____

_____

_____

THE LAST WEEK

☐ **1** Make sure the wedding announcement, with all the necessary information, has gotten to the newspapers.

☐ **2** Put all your wedding clothes (including two pairs of stockings) in one place.

☐ **3** If possible, arrange for someone to be at your house all day on the wedding day to answer telephone calls, keep on eye on gifts, and be on call.

☐ **4** Assemble *everything* you plan to take on your wedding trip. Begin packing.

☐ **5** Check the number of acceptances to the reception and let the club, hotel, or caterer know.

☐ **6** Arrange any last minute transportation details—people to be met at stations or airports, to be picked up for the wedding, and so forth.

☐ **7** Pack your going-away handbag.

☐ **8** Estimate how long it will take you to dress on the day of the wedding. Allow a little extra time for small snags and for picture-taking. Be sure to allow enough time to get to the church on schedule.

☐ **9** Get some tissue paper or a large sheet to protect your dress in the car.

A word of advice! Let others help you. Most people love being part of the preparations for a wedding. If you begin to feel frantic, take an hour off to nap or just sit down and do nothing.

Your Personal Notes:

_____

_____

_____

_____

_____

_____

_____

_____

_____

YOUR WEDDING YOUR WAY

There are hundreds of ways of getting married, ranging from a quiet trip to City Hall to a ceremony on a hilltop to a lavish cathedral wedding. Consider the following guidelines before making your decision. Remember, it's perfectly all right to include the elements of one type of wedding with those of another. But let common sense be your guide. A small wedding with a huge reception—held even a few days or weeks after the ceremony—makes perfect sense; whereas an ultra-formal wedding and a tiny reception aren't compatible. And no doubt you'd feel silly tripping through the fields in a gown with a long train. Whatever your choice, the most important thing is that you feel satisfied and your guests feel comfortable.

THE ULTRA-FORMAL WEDDING

This calls for a fairly large guest list and is almost always held in a church or temple, though occasionally in a ballroom or large home. The invitations, enclosure cards, and announcements are always engraved. The bride wears a traditional long white gown with a train and veil. The groom wears a cutaway (full dress for an evening ceremony). There may be as many as six to twelve bridesmaids, as well as a maid, and possibly matron, of honor, and even one or two child attendants if you like. There is always music: an organist, and in some cases, additional instrumentalists, and a soloist or choir. The ceremony is usually traditional in all respects. Accordingly, the reception is large and elaborate.

THE FORMAL WEDDING

Here the guest list usually ranges between fifty and two hundred. Invitations may be engraved, printed, or handwritten. There are usually two to four bridesmaids (including the honor attendant) and seldom any child attendants. The site is the same as that for an ultra-formal wedding, although the church, club, or home could be smaller. The bridal gown is simpler—traditional, if you like, but with a short train (if any) and a short veil. The groom may wear formal attire (a tuxedo for an evening wedding) or a dark business suit. Often there is no soloist.

THE INFORMAL WEDDING

This is the most flexible type of wedding. It may be held anywhere: church, home, rectory, judge's chambers, or garden. It is usually small, though there is no rule about how many guests or attendants you may have. The bride may wear anything she likes, with or without a head covering. The groom enjoys similar leeway. The invitations are often handwritten or verbal. Generally there is no processional or recessional, and music is optional.

SPECIAL SITUATIONS

A double wedding: Sisters, cousins, or friends often wish to be married at the same ceremony; each bride may act as the other's honor attendant. (See also pages 22 and 38.)

A military wedding: There are many traditions associated with this sort of wedding. The Official Hostess at any of the military academies will be glad to fill you in. Or have your fiancé ask his commanding officer for details.

A second marriage: The status of the bride, not the groom, is the determining factor. If the bride has been married before, she probably would not have a formal wedding, wear a white dress (unless trimmed with color), wear a veil, or send engraved or printed invitations (although announcements are acceptable).

Before you make any definite plans, check with your fiancé. Remember, it's his wedding too.

9

YOUR VISIT TO THE CLERGYMAN

A civil ceremony? Be sure to check with the judge about any special plans you have in mind.

Even if you have no special church affiliation, you may very well decide that you want to be married in a religious rather than a civil ceremony—either in a church or synagogue; at a hotel or club; at home; or possibly in your neighbor's garden or by the side of a lake.

This, of course, means that the service will be performed by a clergyman—and very early in your planning it is essential that you visit him for a preliminary discussion. This meeting is important for many reasons. First, you must find out whether the clergyman is willing to marry you. Even within a particular sect, rules vary widely on such points as whether divorced people may be married, whether interfaith marriages may be performed, and what instances require special dispensations. (When you call to make your appointment, be sure to ask if there are any special documents you should bring along.) Some clergymen also insist upon one or two counseling sessions prior to the ceremony.

There are also a number of practical considerations. Will the church and the clergyman be available on the day and at the time you want to be married? Is the church suitable for the kind of wedding you want? Will the clergyman be willing to marry you elsewhere? When can the rehearsal be scheduled? Are there facilities for the bridal party to dress at the church? Are there any specific church rules about dress? About decorations? May a photographer take pictures inside the church? Is an organist available? Are there any regulations about the kind of music that can be played? About throwing rice? Will the church provide such optional items as kneeling cushions and a canopy, or must you rent them somewhere else? This is also the time for your fiancé to ask about fees.

If you plan to be married at home or somewhere out of doors, ask the clergyman about his preferences. Will he want you to simulate an altar? Does he have any suggestions?

The clergyman may refer you to a secretary or sexton for answers to these practical questions—but only he can confirm his willingness to preside at the ceremony.

YOUR WEDDING YOUR WAY

Not all that long ago, the wording of the marriage ceremony and the type of music that accompanied it were almost unvarying. Today, however, it is not at all uncommon for couples to compose their own versions of the vows they exchange or even the entire ceremony, expressing in a much more personal way exactly how they feel about the commitment they are making. Some couples ask the clergyman to incorporate into the ceremony some readings or thoughts that are especially meaningful to them. Or they may want family and friends to participate in the service. The choice of music may also be highly personal—be it in the instruments, the selections, or both.

In sum, "your wedding your way" may mean a totally traditional ceremony, an entirely innovative one, or one that contains elements of both. But you and your clergyman must agree on this well in advance of the wedding day. And if you feel that your points of view are too widely separated, thank him courteously for his consideration...and find a clergyman who feels more as you do.

WHO PAYS FOR WHAT?

It's not how much you spend but how well you spend it that counts. A warm atmosphere is worth much more than an impersonal show of extravagance.

If there is a limited amount to spend, it's especially important to budget and estimate costs. You may want to cut some corners but not others. For instance, a generous service of punch is preferable to a skimpy service of vintage champagne. And field flowers in profusion can be far more beautiful than one or two stiffly structured professional arrangements. Moreover, a wedding that you've "done" yourself can be the most meaningful. To sew your own dress, bake your own cake, or have a small at-home reception makes very special memories. A reception with homemade refreshments is more work, to be sure, but it often has a charm that catered affairs lack. And the helping hands of family and friends are sure to be among the most memorable gifts you receive. (Menus and recipes for receptions you can handle yourself begin on page 45.)

In the past the expenses of a wedding and reception were strictly divided among the various participants: The bride's family always paid for this, the groom's family always paid for that. Today the lines are much less rigidly drawn, so even in matters of money you may have your wedding your way. If you work, you may want to take on a number of the expenses that the bride's family traditionally assumes. Or you and your fiancé may save jointly to cover most or all of the costs involved. The groom's family may discreetly offer to supply the wine or underwrite the entire reception if they are in a better position to do so. Let common sense be your guide.

Traditionally, however, this is how the expenses have been divided:

THE BRIDE OR HER FAMILY PAYS FOR

All invitations, announcements, and enclosures
All photographs (wedding and reception)
The flowers for all members of the wedding party
All wedding ceremony expenses (flowers, candles, canopy, cars, special music, etc.)
All reception expenses (rental of hotel, club, or restaurant; food and drink; help; flowers; musicians; etc.)
The bride's wedding dress, trousseau, and going-away outfit

They sometimes also pay for
Hotel accommodations for the bridesmaids
The bridesmaids' dresses

THE BRIDE PAYS FOR

Her gift to the groom
The groom's ring (if any)
Gifts for her attendants

THE GROOM PAYS FOR

The marriage license
His gift to the bride
The bride's ring
The clergyman's fee
Gifts for his attendants
The wedding trip

He sometimes also pays for
The bride's bouquet and going-away corsage, corsages for mothers and grandmothers, boutonnieres for his attendants and both fathers (It's easier if the bride orders all the flowers.)

THE GROOM'S FAMILY PAYS FOR

Their own hotel accommodations (if any)
Rehearsal dinner (if they give one)
Their clothes for the wedding

They sometimes also pay for
Hotel accommodations for the best man and ushers
Accessories and rental of clothes for the best man and ushers

11

KEEPING TRACK OF COSTS

Stationery
[Include invitations, announcements, at-home cards, note paper, postage, etc.]

	Estimate	Actual
Total	$	$

Bridal Costume
[Include dress, veil, shoes, etc.]

	Estimate	Actual
Total	$	$

Transportation
[Include limousines, police, misc.]

	Estimate	Actual
Total	$	$

Photographs
[Include portraits, album, candids, glossies for newspaper.]

	Estimate	Actual
Total	$	$

Flowers
[Include church, reception, bouquets, corsages, etc.]

	Estimate	Actual
Total	$	$

KEEPING TRACK OF COSTS

Ceremony
[Include church fees, music, canopy, etc.]

	Estimate	Actual
_____	_____	_____
_____	_____	_____
_____	_____	_____
_____	_____	_____
_____	_____	_____
Total	$ _____	$ _____

Reception
[Include rental, music, food, drink, other services.]

	Estimate	Actual
_____	_____	_____
_____	_____	_____
_____	_____	_____
_____	_____	_____
_____	_____	_____
_____	_____	_____
_____	_____	_____
_____	_____	_____
_____	_____	_____
_____	_____	_____
_____	_____	_____
_____	_____	_____
_____	_____	_____
_____	_____	_____
_____	_____	_____
_____	_____	_____
_____	_____	_____
_____	_____	_____
Total	$ _____	$ _____

Presents
[Include gifts for groom, attendants, hostesses, etc.]

	Estimate	Actual
_____	_____	_____
_____	_____	_____
_____	_____	_____
_____	_____	_____
_____	_____	_____
_____	_____	_____
_____	_____	_____
Total	$ _____	$ _____

Other

	Estimate	Actual
_____	_____	_____
_____	_____	_____
_____	_____	_____
_____	_____	_____
_____	_____	_____
_____	_____	_____
_____	_____	_____
_____	_____	_____
_____	_____	_____
_____	_____	_____
_____	_____	_____
_____	_____	_____
_____	_____	_____
_____	_____	_____
_____	_____	_____
_____	_____	_____
_____	_____	_____
Total	$ _____	$ _____

YOUR ATTENDANTS

Keep track of your attendants—their sizes and such—on pages 16 and 17.

You and your fiancé choose your attendants from among family and close friends, often mixing the two families—his sister as one of your bridesmaids, your brother as an usher. Even the smallest ceremony calls for two attendants as witnesses, usually a maid of honor and a best man. In a larger ceremony there are usually more (see page 9), and often there are more ushers than bridesmaids (there should be one usher for every fifty guests).

Think about how you'll arrange your attendants in the processional and recessional. Will the bridesmaids walk singly or in pairs? Which usher will escort which bridesmaid? Would one more usher or bridesmaid help to balance the bridal table? (See pages 37 and 41.)

WHAT YOUR ATTENDANTS DO

Maid or matron of honor. She precedes you, the bride, and your father in the processional (unless there is a flower girl or ring-bearer); she attends you at the altar, holding the bouquet and groom's ring, putting back the face veil and arranging the train for the recessional. Afterward she signs the marriage license as a legal witness. At the reception she stands in the receiving line. Later she helps you dress for your wedding trip. If you have both a maid and a matron of honor, decide which one will attend you at the altar; she will follow the other in the processional.

Bridesmaids. Their role is primarily decorative and supportive. In the processional they walk individually or in pairs. In the recessional they may repeat the pattern or be paired with ushers. The bridesmaids stand in the receiving line. Junior bridesmaids (ages eight to fourteen) have the same duties as bridesmaids.

The bridesmaids' dresses are meant to create a pretty, colorful picture at the ceremony and in the receiving line. They should be consistent with the tone of the bride's gown—equally formal or informal. Bridesmaids dress more or less identically, though the maid or matron of honor may wear a different color, and a very young junior bridesmaid's dress may be a more youthful version of the others'. Shoes are usually dyed to match the dresses; gloves and head coverings are optional. Although the mothers of the bride and groom are not participants in the ceremony, their dresses should be equally formal and color-coordinated.

Best man. He is usually a brother or best friend of the groom and acts as a legal witness. He must be a man you can depend on. He takes charge of the ring and marriage license, helps the groom dress and pack, and generally lends moral support—especially just before the ceremony. He also "mother hens" the ushers, making sure that they arrive on time for the rehearsal and ceremony and checking to see that they are properly dressed. He also returns any rented clothes after the wedding. Just before the ceremony he hands the clergyman his fee in a sealed envelope. At the reception the best man proposes the first toast to the bride and groom. Before leave-taking he helps the groom dress; he also arranges for the car in which the newly married couple will leave the reception. So, much as a sixteen-year-old brother would love to be best man, he'd have a much better time as an usher.

Ushers. Their main job is to seat the wedding guests. At a church wedding they escort all women guests to their pews, asking, "Are you a friend of the bride or groom?" (The bride's friends and family sit on the left, the groom's on the right.) The woman's escort follows a few steps behind. When several women arrive in a group and it is impossible to escort each one, the usher offers his right arm to the senior woman, and the others follow. A male guest simply follows the usher to the pew. For a large wedding one usher is designated head usher. Just before the ceremony is about to begin, he first seats the groom's mother (right-hand front pew) and then the bride's mother (left-hand front pew). After the ceremony, before any guests leave the church, he escorts the mothers out in reverse order. At a very formal wedding two ushers stretch the white aisle ribbons and unroll the aisle carpet just before the processional.

At a home or outdoor wedding where there is no formal seating, the ushers merely mix with the guests and make sure that no one is left standing alone. They do not stand in the receiving line at the reception but again keep their eyes open for anyone in need of company.

All male members of the wedding party—the groom, best man, ushers, and father of the bride—dress identically. At an ultra-formal wedding they may wear cutaways and striped trousers in the morning or afternoon, tuxedos or (very formally) white ties and tailcoats in the evening. For a less formal or an informal wedding they will probably wear dark business suits—all the same color—and white shirts. Their ties (plain, striped, or print) should be the same or similar. Since few young men today own tuxedos or cutaways, formal wedding attire is usually rented (all from the same place to insure uniformity). You or your fiancé should line up a reputable rental firm and look at its stock. Ideally, all the men should try on the suits for correct fit. If this is impossible—and it often is—ask them to send their measurements to you or the groom so you can make the necessary reservations (about six weeks before the wedding).

Flower girl. She walks immediately in front of the bride in the processional and often carries a basket of flower petals to strew along the aisle. Her dress may be of the same color and fabric as the bridesmaids', or it may be a white party frock. The flower girl does not stand in the receiving line.

Ring-bearer. He is usually no older than six. In the processional he precedes the flower girl (if there is one) and carries a white satin cushion to which the ring (the real one or a facsimile) is lightly stitched. He usually wears white and, like the flower girl, does not stand in the receiving line.

WHAT YOU DO FOR THEM

Choose dresses that appeal to you, of course, but be sure to consider each girl's size, coloring, and tastes. Be considerate about costs, and try to select a style that can be worn again.

Arrange for any fittings. This may require a good deal of dovetailing if your attendants are spread throughout the country.

Pick out the bridesmaids' shoes and arrange to have them dyed. The shoes can actually be purchased at different stores, but they should all be dyed at the same place and time.

Tell them what jewelry to wear.

Keep them posted on the times and places for fittings, parties, photographs, and dressing on the day of the wedding.

Give each attendant a gift (see page 35).

Provide escorts to prewedding parties. (Single ushers should do the honors.)

If any of your attendants are from out of town, make hotel reservations or house-guest plans for them.

Arrange for their transportation to the ceremony and the reception.

Remind your fiancé to make similar arrangements for his attendants.

The head usher should be able to recognize most of the guests. Therefore, it's a bit difficult for an out-of-towner to assume this responsibility.

HIS WEDDING HIS WAY

The groom, as well as the bride, has many options in today's wedding. He may choose to wear something much more colorful than the conventional formal wear or business suit: a velvet Edwardian suit with an elaborately ruffled shirt, a Mexican wedding shirt, a paisley scarf, or anything else that reflects his particular tastes—and that complements the style of your dress. The best man and ushers then dress accordingly, though not necessarily identically.

15

NOTES ON ATTENDANTS

Maid of Honor _____

Address _____

Telephone _____

Dress size _____ Shoe size _____ Head size _____

Notes: _____

_____

Best Man _____

Address _____

Telephone _____

Jacket size _____

Trousers: Waist _____ Outside Seam _____

Inside Seam _____

Shirt: Neck _____ Sleeve _____

Notes: _____

_____

Bride's Father _____

Jacket size _____

Trousers: Waist _____ Outside Seam _____

Inside Seam _____

Shirt: Neck _____ Sleeve _____

Notes: _____

_____

Bridesmaid _____

Address _____

Telephone _____

Dress size _____ Shoe size _____ Head size _____

Notes: _____

_____

Bridesmaid _____

Address _____

Telephone _____

Dress size _____ Shoe size _____ Head size _____

Notes: _____

_____

Bridesmaid _____

Address _____

Telephone _____

Dress size _____ Shoe size _____ Head size _____

Notes: _____

_____

Bridesmaid _____

Address _____

Telephone _____

Dress size _____ Shoe size _____ Head size _____

Notes: _____

_____

Bridesmaid _____

Address _____

Telephone _____

Dress size _____ Shoe size _____ Head size _____

Notes: _____

_____

Flower Girl _____

Parents' names _____

Address _____

Telephone _____

Notes: _____

NOTES ON ATTENDANTS

Usher _____

Address _____

Telephone _____

Jacket size _____

Trousers: Waist _____ Outside Seam _____

      Inside Seam _____

Shirt: Neck _____ Sleeve _____

Notes: _____

Usher _____

Address _____

Telephone _____

Jacket size _____

Trousers: Waist _____ Outside Seam _____

      Inside Seam _____

Shirt: Neck _____ Sleeve _____

Notes: _____

Usher _____

Address _____

Telephone _____

Jacket size _____

Trousers: Waist _____ Outside Seam _____

      Inside Seam _____

Shirt: Neck _____ Sleeve _____

Notes: _____

Groom's Parents _____

Address _____

Telephone _____

Notes: _____

_____

Usher _____

Address _____

Telephone _____

Jacket size _____

Trousers: Waist _____ Outside Seam _____

      Inside Seam _____

Shirt: Neck _____ Sleeve _____

Notes: _____

Usher _____

Address _____

Telephone _____

Jacket size _____

Trousers: Waist _____ Outside Seam _____

      Inside Seam _____

Shirt: Neck _____ Sleeve _____

Notes: _____

Usher _____

Address _____

Telephone _____

Jacket size _____

Trousers: Waist _____ Outside Seam _____

      Inside Seam _____

Shirt: Neck _____ Sleeve _____

Notes: _____

Ring-bearer _____

Parents' names _____

Address _____

Telephone _____

Notes: _____

YOUR GUEST LIST

If you have done your budgeting realistically, you should have a fairly clear idea of exactly how many people you will be able to invite. And unless you've decided on a very large and very expensive wedding, the difficult task now becomes pruning down the list of all the people you know and would like to invite to a number that fits into your initial figuring.

The allotment for the groom's family. Technically, half of the guest list is allotted to the groom's family; however, it seldom works out that way in practice—unless the families live nearby. In reality, the bride's family usually invites the majority of guests in attendance. But you can't set a hard-and-fast rule about this. So much depends on the personalities and circumstances involved.

Let's say you've decided on 150 guests for the reception. Immediately call or write the groom's mother and tell her of your plans. Ask her to send you a list of about 75 people she'd like you to invite (proportionately fewer if you and your fiancé are making a separate list of your own friends). If your budget permits, be somewhat flexible about the number. Ask if you may have her list, with full names and complete addresses, by a specific date. And remember to ask for a list of those who should get announcements. If your fiancé's family lives some distance away, you might also ask for an estimate of how many acceptances you're likely to get.

The musts on your list. Unless you are having the smallest of weddings or a civil ceremony there are some people who custom dictates must be invited to both wedding and reception. These include the wives, husbands, or fiancés of the members of your wedding party; the clergyman (and his wife); any brothers or sisters (and their wives or husbands) of both bride and groom. List all of these first, remembering not to count a couple or family as a single unit. Now see how many places are left over.

Get the proper equipment. If your guest list numbers fifty or fewer, you can keep the necessary records in a small notebook. If it's larger, your task will be easier if you use a file box with cards, dividers, and an alphabetical index. On each card write, or preferably type, the name of each guest or guests (use one card per family, including children's names) and the address. Note clearly whether the guest is to get an invitation to the ceremony, to the reception, or both; also list those who are to receive only an announcement (in fact, you may wish to divide the cards into corresponding groups). The cards for those invited to the reception should also have space for the date sent, for the acceptance or regret, and for the number attending (see the sample below). For quick tallying, group the cards noting acceptances together.

Later you can use the back of each card for making notations about wedding gifts, including a brief description of the gift, the date received, the store, and the date acknowledged.

Even after you've acknowledged all the gifts, this file can prove useful to you as a permanent personal address file and a reminder to mention the gift sometime again in the future.

```
CEREMONY AND RECEPTION

                    Mr. and Mrs. John Morris
                    3169 Stanwood Lane
                    Lafayette, Calif.   94549

                    (Nancy and John)

Sent  7/9
Accepted  7/24
Regretted  —
No. Attending  (4)
```

YOUR WEDDING INVITATIONS

As soon as you have established the size of your guest list, it's time to seek out a knowledgeable stationer (more about this on page 25), choose your invitations and announcements, and get an estimate on costs and delivery dates. It's important to get this done early because engraving will take at least ten days (printing can be delivered more quickly); and depending on the length of your list, the demands on your time, and how many helpers you can enlist, addressing the invitations can mean a matter of days or weeks. To help you get a head start on this job, ask to have the envelopes delivered separately and early. With luck, you'll be finished with your addressing by the time the invitations and announcements are delivered. (Three months before the wedding is not too early to do your ordering—if your plans are definite.)

FORMAL INVITATIONS

Paper: A wide variety of paper stock is available. ("Stock" refers to the quality of the paper and how heavy or thin it is.) Traditionally the paper is white or ivory.

Style: All formal invitations are folded sheets, with the engraving on the front. They are available in two sizes: one 5 by 7¼ inches, which is often folded a second time before being inserted into the envelope, and a smaller size, 4½ x 5½ inches, that fits the envelope exactly. Both come with a sheet of tissue over the engraving to prevent smudging. (The tissue should be left on.) The larger double-size invitation is more expensive and usually used for very formal weddings, but the smaller invitation is just as correct.

Lettering: Engraving is the traditional and most opulent form of lettering. The text of the invitation is first etched on a copper plate, which in itself is relatively expensive. A great many reproductions can be made from a single plate, however, so the more invitations you order, the less they cost per copy. Usually the minimum number an engraver will handle is one hundred.

There is also a method of raised printing which looks superficially like engraving. This is less expensive, particularly if you are ordering in small numbers, and your invitations can be delivered in a matter of a few days. If your budget is tight, your list is small, or your time is short, you may want to consider this method. You might think about handwritten notes too (see page 22).

There are a number of typefaces available, ranging from modern to traditional. Choose the one that best reflects the "feeling" you have about your wedding.

Envelopes: All formal invitations come with two envelopes, an inner one and an outer one. The outer envelope is gummed and carries the full names of the guests—"Mr. and Mrs. Archibald Mayes Brooks"—and the address. The inner envelope, slightly smaller, is not gummed and is simply addressed to "Mr. and Mrs. Brooks"—no first names, no address. (See the chart on page 20 for more about addressing inner envelopes.)

Insertion of invitations into envelopes: The fold of the inserted invitation should be placed at the bottom of the inner envelope so that the lettering faces the flap. Any enclosures—at-home cards and the like (see page 25)—should be inside the fold of the invitation, whether single or double fold, so they will not be overlooked and thrown away with the envelope. Most stationers recommend that the inner envelope, holding the invitation, be inserted into the outer envelope in such a way that the name

Send extra invitations and announcements to the groom's family. They'll want them for keepsakes.

19

on the front of the inner envelope is upright and faces the flap of the outer envelope.

Return address: This should be embossed on the flap of the envelope so that any undeliverable invitations will be returned. Your stationer can arrange for the embossing, or you can get a home embosser made up with your address and do the job yourself. Just remember that this is another time-consuming task, making it even more important to have the outer envelopes delivered to you as early as possible.

Addressing invitations: Use blue or black ink. If your handwriting is not as pretty as you'd like or if it's unclear, recruit members of the family or friends with attractive handwriting to do the job. (Or your stationer can probably give you the name of someone who does this professionally.)

The addressing should always be formal. That means:

Use no abbreviations except "Mr.," "Mrs.," "Dr.," and "Jr." Other titles, such as "Colonel," "Reverend," "Senator," and the like, should be written out.

Some women prefer the title "Ms." to "Mrs." or "Miss." Do not use this form of address unless you know that the woman feels strongly about it. In the case of a divorcée or widow, use her given name with "Ms."—not "Ms. Foster Evans" or "Ms. Charles Green." And never, never "Mr. and Ms."

Write names in full—no initials and no nicknames. If you don't know what an initial stands for, omit it.

Write out "and" between titles: "Dr. *and* Mrs."

Do not use the phrase "and family." If you are inviting a family, use only the parents' name on the outer envelope. The children's names appear on a separate line on the inner envelope (see the chart below).

Write out directions such as "East."

Write out "Avenue," "Street," "Drive," and so forth.

Write out all numbers except house numbers: "108 East Eighty-second Street." Figures may be used for high-numbered streets, however: "107-61 West 117th Street."

Use zip codes whenever possible.

FORMS OF ADDRESS FOR INNER AND OUTER ENVELOPES

	Inner Envelope	*Outer Envelope*
To a husband and wife	Mr. and Mrs. Stuart	Mr. and Mrs. James Stuart
To a number of children (under twenty-one) included in their parents' invitation	Mr. and Mrs. Gardella Ann, Margaret, and John [in order of age]	Mr. and Mrs. George Gardella
To a teen-age girl included in her parents' invitation	Mr. and Mrs. Shean Miss Nancy	Mr. and Mrs. David Shean
To a boy included in his parents' invitation	Mr. and Mrs. Rice Ralph	Mr. and Mrs. Arthur Rice
To a divorced woman	Mrs. Evans	Mrs. Foster Evans [a combination of her maiden name and her former husband's surname]
To a widow	Mrs. Green	Mrs. Charles Green [her deceased husband's name]

Note: All adults living at the same address should receive separate invitations (except, of course, a husband and wife, who receive only one).

Mailing: Send the invitations by first-class mail three to four weeks before the wedding —earlier and by airmail if they are going out of the country.

Mishaps: If an invitation is returned because of an incorrect address or if you slipped up on sending someone an invitation, telephone the minute the error is discovered—no matter how late. Explain the mistake and tell the person how much you hope he will still be able to come to the wedding, even on such short notice.

The wording: Here's an example of the typical wording for a formal invitation to a church wedding:

Mr. and Mrs. Charles Donald Burns
request the honour of your presence
at the marriage of their daughter
Mary Ellen
to
Mr. Thomas Laidlaw Newman
on Saturday, the eighth of June
One thousand nine hundred and seventy-four
at half after four o'clock
Saint Anne's Church
Dayton, Ohio

Common variations: The wording may vary according to local customs or special circumstances:

For a home, club, or hotel wedding "the pleasure of your company" is substituted for "the honour of your presence."

The year may be expressed "Nineteen hundred and seventy-four" instead of "One thousand nine hundred and seventy-four." (The year need not be cited in an invitation.)

If the church is not well known or the wedding is held at home, the street address should be included.

If the city is very large, the state need not be mentioned.

If a Catholic marriage takes place during a nuptial mass, this is often noted on the invitation: "at a ten o'clock Nuptial Mass." (Consult the priest and stationer for other possible variations in wording.)

If formal invitations are being issued for a second marriage, the bride would use her married name: "Mary Ellen Chase" if widowed, "Mary Burns Chase" if divorced.

YOUR WEDDING YOUR WAY

If you're planning a wedding tailored more to your personal feelings than to convention, you may very well want to express this in your invitation and announcement. And as long as the tone is appropriate, the words may be whatever you choose. Perhaps: "Mr. and Mrs. James Farrow wish to share their joy in the marriage of their daughter...." Or you might like to include the names of the groom's parents, along with those of your own, as a mark of affection:

Mr. and Mrs. James Farrow
and
Mr. and Mrs. Henry Martin, III
request the honour of your presence
at the marriage of their children
Constance Phoebe Farrow
and
Stephen Henry Martin . . .

If you like, the invitations may be on a tinted paper, or the lettering may be in color. The dimensions may vary too. If you're artistically inclined, you might want to do the lettering by hand or create a special design.

Note the use of the British spellings of "honour" and "favour" in a formal invitation.

WHO ISSUES THE INVITATIONS?

The bride's parents sponsor the wedding, and their names appear on the invitation: "Mr. and Mrs. Jefferson Conway McAlpin request ..." (see full text at left). But there are, of course, exceptions:

If one parent has died and the other has not remarried, the single father or mother sends the invitation: "Mr. [or Mrs.] Frank Sinclair Smith requests...."

If a widowed parent has remarried, the invitation is issued jointly, but the bride is referred to as "his daughter" or "her daughter."

If the parents are separated, they usually issue invitations jointly as "Mr. and Mrs."

If the parents are divorced but both are living, it is customary for the mother to issue the

21

invitation. (The father often hosts the reception, issuing separate reception invitations in his name.) If she has remarried, the invitations are usually issued in her name and that of her second husband:

Mr. and Mrs. Martin Lee McDonald
request the honour of your presence
at the marriage of her daughter
[or "at the marriage of Mrs. McDonald's daughter"]
Jane Anne Plotner . . .

But if the bride has been living with her father and his second wife, they would issue the invitation and the wording would be "his daughter" (or "Mr. Plotner's daughter"). If divorced parents choose to issue a joint invitation, they would follow the form outlined on page 24.

If neither parent is living, the invitation may be issued by any close relative, in which case the wording would read "her granddaughter," "his niece," or whatever is appropriate.

If the sponsor of the wedding is not a relative, the wording is changed slightly:

Mr. Lathrop Matthews, Jr.
requests the honour of your presence
at the marriage of
Miss Valerie Anne Benedict . . .

The use of "Miss" indicates that there is no blood relationship.

If the bride issues the invitations herself, the correct wording would be:

The honour of your presence
is requested at the marriage of
Miss Valerie Ann Benedict
to
Dr. Thomas Allan Roth . . .

SPECIAL SITUATIONS

A double wedding: If the brides are sisters, the invitation is always issued jointly:

Mrs. Manning Johnson
requests the pleasure of your company
at the marriage of her daughters
Sarah Louise
to
Mr. Arthur Louis Phelan, III
and
Jennifer
to
Dr. Samuel Trent Glazer . . .

If the brides are cousins or friends, the families usually send separate invitations.

A military wedding: The invitation to a military wedding differs only in its treatment of the groom's title. But there are so many variables, from rank to rank and service to service, that it is best to get the advice of a well-versed stationer or your fiancé's commanding officer. In general, a junior officer's rank and branch of service appear below his name:

John William Nolan
Second Lieutenant, United States Marine Corps

An enlisted man's name would be treated similarly, but he has the option to omit his rank. A senior officer uses his rank as his title ("Captain Robert Vrooman"); he can dispense with the line denoting his service affiliation.

INFORMAL INVITATIONS

When a wedding is small (fifty people or fewer), a second marriage for the bride, a marriage of older people; if the wedding date is set on short notice; or if there has been a death, separation, or other problem in the family, the wedding is almost always informal (see page 9). In such cases the invitations should be handwritten by the bride's mother or the bride herself (not helpful friends). They should be written in blue or black ink on plain white or ivory paper or on small informals, with or without an engraved name or monogram. For example, a note from the bride's mother might read:

Dear Terry and Peter,
   Cathie and Wayne Rodgers are being married on Wednesday, the sixteenth of this month. We hope you can join us for a small ceremony in the chapel at the First Presbyterian Church in Oakland and then come to the house to celebrate. The ceremony is at 5:30, and having you there will make it that much happier for all of us.
                    Love,
                    Marguerite Smith

If time does not permit the writing of notes, it is quite acceptable to telephone the invitations. And even the groom may participate, calling his own friends.

YOUR RECEPTION INVITATIONS

FORMAL RECEPTION INVITATIONS

If everyone being invited to the wedding is also being invited to the reception (the most prevalent practice today), the reception invitations can be incorporated into the wedding invitations. Immediately after the name and address of the place where the ceremony will be performed, the following lines are added:

and afterward at the reception
Indian Head Country Club
100 Indian Lane

(If the town is not the same as the one in which the ceremony will take place, it too should be included.)

If the reception is at home, the lines read:

and afterward at the reception
850 East Ridgewood Road
Easton, Iowa

In the lower left-hand corner of such an invitation a request for acknowledgment is included. This may read: "R.s.v.p." or "The favour of a reply is requested."

If the reception is being held at a club or hotel, the bride's parents' home address (including the zip code) should follow this request. No address is necessary for a home reception, since the address has already been given in the body of the invitation.

If more people are being invited to the wedding than to the reception, the reception invitation is engraved on a separate enclosure card:

Reception
immediately following the ceremony
White Plains Hotel
Please reply to 333 West Allendale Road

If the wedding ceremony is to be small and the reception larger (sometimes even given on another day), the order reverses itself. The larger invitation is for the reception alone, and the enclosure card is used to invite the more limited list of guests to the ceremony. In this case the reception invitation reads:

Mr. and Mrs. John Jay Lee
request the pleasure of your company
at the wedding reception of their daughter
["wedding breakfast" if it's held before one o'clock]
Mary Jane
and
[note, in this case, not "to"]
Mr. Jason Philip Kaplan
Saturday, the fourth of August
at four o'clock
Margate Country Club
Weston, Massachusetts

R.s.v.p.
167 School Street
Milton, Massachusetts 02186

The smaller enclosure card would then read:

Ceremony
at three o'clock
[include date if not the same as the reception]
First Congregational Church
Milton, Massachusetts

INFORMAL RECEPTION INVITATIONS

An invitation to an informal reception is usually part of the wedding invitation (see page 22). But if your plans call for a large party after a very small ceremony—even some weeks after the ceremony—simply use your own words in a note.

Dear Len,

Greg and I are being married a week from Saturday, on the nineteenth, and we're having a little party to celebrate after the ceremony. We do hope you can join us at Mother's house around five for cake and champagne. It won't really seem official without you.

Love,
Gloria

*Awaiting R.S.V.P.s?
Go ahead and call if
the deadline is at hand.
Mail can go astray.*

YOUR ANNOUNCEMENTS, ENCLOSURES, & STATIONERY

WEDDING ANNOUNCEMENTS

A formal wedding announcement is a way of letting friends and acquaintances who were not invited to the wedding know that the happy event has indeed taken place. They are never sent to anyone invited to the wedding or reception. Announcements are usually the size of a small wedding invitation, and they, too, are enclosed in two envelopes and addressed formally (see pages 19-20).

Announcements are addressed in advance and mailed after the wedding—on the same day or on the following day. (Among many other superstitions connected with weddings is one that holds that it is bad luck to mail announcements before the ceremony has actually occurred.) There is no firm rule about when announcements are sent out, however, and in the case of an elopement or a secret marriage they may be dispatched weeks or even months after the event.

If the wedding is to be a small one, the list of people to receive announcements may be limited to relatives and friends—those who probably would have been invited had the ceremony been larger. Or the list may be much longer, including more casual friends, distant relatives, business acquaintances, former schoolteachers—indeed, anyone who would be happy to receive an announcement. The beauty of the wedding announcement is that it is a gracious gesture, pure and simple, carrying no obligation on the part of the recipient to send a gift or even a note of acknowledgment.

Announcements may also be sent by anyone regardless of the circumstances of the marriage—civil ceremony, marriage of a divorcée or widow, or whatever.

The form of an engraved announcement is very similar to that of a wedding invitation and follows most of the same rules. A typical announcement made by the parents of the bride would read:

Dr. and Mrs. Amos Bell
have the honour to announce
the marriage of their daughter
Valerie Susan
to
Mr. George Marshall Harris
on Tuesday, the fourth of December
One thousand nine hundred and seventy-three
Brick Presbyterian Church
New York City

Common variations: The wording may vary as follows:

"Have the honour of announcing" may be used instead of "have the honour to announce."

The date may be expressed "Nineteen hundred and seventy-three" instead of "One thousand nine hundred and seventy-three." (The year is always included in an announcement.)

If the city is small, add the name of the state.

The place where the ceremony took place may be omitted.

If the bride is a widow or divorcée, her married surname would be used: "Valerie Bell Lloyd" if a divorcée, "Valerie Susan Lloyd" if a widow.

Issuing the announcements: A wedding announcement is made by the bride's parents or by the same person or persons who issue the wedding invitation (see pages 21-22). Although divorced parents seldom issue a joint invitation, they often choose to issue the announcement together.

Mrs. George Bridges
and
Mr. Thomas Acton
have the honour to announce . . .

AT-HOME CARDS

If you are going to be living somewhere other than your home city, it is a convenience to friends to include an at-home card with the announcement, stating your new address and the date on which you expect to take up residence. The card, which should match the paper and type style of the announcement, is placed inside the fold:

At home
after the eighteenth of December
680 Harmon Avenue
Dallas, Texas 75229

or

Mr. and Mrs. Robert Schiffman
99 Seneca Street
Westwood Park, New Jersey 07675
after the sixth of July

At-home cards are usually not included with an invitation; instead, they may be sent separately after the wedding.

MAPS

If either the wedding or the reception (or both) is to be held at a location that might be difficult for people to find, it is perfectly proper to enclose with the invitation a small map indicating the route to take from a main highway or a conspicuous landmark. Such maps are printed, not engraved. They are sometimes supplied by establishments that cater to weddings and receptions, or you can ask a talented friend to draw the route. The stationer will have the maps printed for you.

REPLY CARDS

The custom of including a reply card with a reception invitation, though not correct in the traditional sense, has become fairly common today. If such a card is enclosed, the person receiving it should, of course, use it to reply.

YOUR STATIONER

All invitations, announcements, and enclosure cards are available from a stationer—and in many instances from the stationery department of a department store or large jeweler. It's a good idea to choose the most distinguished firm in your area; prices for a given quality of paper and engraving vary only slightly, and a knowledgeable stationer can be an invaluable source of advice. He will have dozens of samples of all kinds so you can see exactly what you are ordering; if there are any unusual circumstances that call for variant wording, he can tell you the proper way to handle it. If your list is long or time is short, he may be able to refer you to a professional who will address the invitations and announcements for you. He can supply you with:

Wedding and reception invitations
Announcements
Enclosures
Notepaper for thank-you notes (written before the wedding)
Informals with your married name or monogram
Formal letter paper
Everyday stationery, with your name and address printed (not engraved) on it

The stationer can also take care of any printed materials you may need for your reception: matchbooks, napkins, guest book. He may also be able to arrange for place cards and boxes for the groom's cake.

Monogramming: A monogram consists of your three initials: the first letters of your given name, your maiden surname, and your married surname. These may be arranged in two different orders, depending on the type of lettering used. If the lettering is script, the initial of your married surname is larger than the other two and appears between them. If the monogram is in block letters, they are all the same size and the initial of the married surname is last. Thus, the monogram for Carolyn Dixon Long would be:

Your stationer will have a wide range of styles to choose from. Remember that the die from which engravings are made may be used for many years and on many different sizes of letter paper, so choose a type style that will be appropriate for many kinds of stationery.

YOUR NEWSPAPER ANNOUNCEMENTS

Watch your local paper for an announcement you like and use it as your guide.

It's almost certain that there are people outside of your immediate circle who are interested in news about you, so you and your family may very well want to announce your engagement, your wedding, or both in the newspaper.

Check the paper's requirements. Well in advance of the day you want the announcement to appear, telephone the newspaper and ask whether there is a special way they want the information presented. (Some papers supply forms for you to fill out.) Find out what their deadline is for the particular issue (it may be weeks in advance) and what kind of photograph, if any, they prefer. If your fiancé's family lives in another town, ask his mother to check out the requirements for their local paper.

Provide full and accurate information. The required data generally includes the full names of you and your fiancé (no nicknames), your parents' names (if someone else is making the announcement, see page 22), the names of the groom's parents and the city where they live, and the date and place of the wedding. You might also include the schools you have both attended, your professional affiliations, and the business connections of both fathers (mothers, too) if they are prominent. Be sure to specify the date of the issue in which the announcement should appear. Type the information and triple check the spellings of all names. Be sure to include your telephone number so the information can be verified or augmented if necessary.

Don't worry about the exact wording. All papers have their own styles and will word your notice accordingly (alas—however strongly you feel about your own phrasing). Some newspapers include only the bare essentials, others verge on life histories. A typical engagement announcement might read:

Mr. and Mrs. Lowell Gary Sheehan, of 823 Oakdale Drive [or "of this city"], announce the engagement of their daughter, Susan Ann, to Mr. Frank Mansfield Roberts, son of Mr. and Mrs. Samuel Grey Roberts, of Dallas, Texas. Miss Thomas was graduated from Lynnehurst High School and attended Wells College. [The term "attended" is used when a student was not graduated from a particular school.] Mr. Roberts is a graduate of the University of Colorado and is now associated with the engineering firm of Wadley and Lytell in this city. The wedding will take place in June [or "no date has been set for the wedding"].

A wedding announcement covers the same information, though of course it's worded to include the time and place of the wedding. It may also contain the names of wedding attendants, the officiating clergyman, where you are going on your wedding trip, and where you plan to live.

Note: If the bride has been married before, there is rarely an engagement announcement. It is quite correct, however, to announce the wedding after it has taken place.

YOUR WEDDING YOUR WAY

Newspapers in some cities are now using photographs that include the groom for both the engagement and the wedding announcements. If you and your fiancé have a suitable picture that you'd like to use, ask if it may be substituted for the more conventional bride's portrait.

YOUR WEDDING DRESS & TROUSSEAU

YOUR WEDDING DRESS

Here you have the widest possible choice. The only rule today seems to be to choose a gown that's consistent with the other details of your wedding.

Start your shopping early. Virtually all wedding dresses are made to order, which means a minimum of eight weeks from the time you make your selection to the time the dress leaves the manufacturer. And you'll want to allow at least another two weeks for fittings at the store. (A word of caution: Don't have your final fitting too early in the game. Many brides experience surprising weight gains or losses as they cope with prewedding activities.) Keep in mind, too, that most sample bridal gowns reach the shops about six months ahead of time, so the earlier you shop, the wider your selection.

To save time, have a good idea of how much you want to spend and the type of dress you want to wear before you even set foot in a store. Will you want something storybook traditional? Traditional but timely? Or a dress that's truly avant-garde?

Will you want a headpiece with a veil? Or will you opt instead for flowers, ribbons, or perhaps a bonnet or kerchief? Decide on your headpiece when you order your dress. Think about purely practical matters, too. Does the dress require special undergarments: a long slip, a strapless bra, a waist-nipper?

If you buy your dress at a bridal shop or in the bridal department of a large store, avail yourself of any extra services that are offered. Many stores offer discounts on flowers and photographs; some even provide personal assistance on the day of the wedding.

For a formal wedding, a long dress in satin, lace, or any luxurious fabric and some sort of veil is the norm. Traditionally, a formal wedding gown is white or ivory, but it is quite proper to choose a pastel, or for a winter wedding, a deep jewel-tone velvet; even prints are worn occasionally. Sleeves may be long or short; gloves and a train are optional.

Shoes are usually silk or satin (or linen in the summer) and match the dress. Stockings are light colored but not white.

If you wear long gloves, carefully slit the stitching of the third finger, left hand, so that the wedding ring may be slipped on easily. A short glove may be removed.

For a less formal wedding, the options are much the same, though a long veil or train might seem a bit pretentious.

For an informal wedding, anything becoming is appropriate.

YOUR TROUSSEAU

A trousseau is, quite simply, whatever clothes you take with you, not merely on your wedding trip but also into your new life. Spend some time going over the contents of your closet, checking to see that everything is clean and any necessary alterations have been made. Then decide what gaps need to be filled.

CLOTHES FOR YOUR WEDDING TRIP

Quite possibly you and your fiancé have decided to spend your honeymoon in a place as different as possible from the one you live in: a Caribbean island, a camp pitched in the wilderness, or the Swiss Alps. Certain things, like a hairbrush and medications, are musts. Others depend on the weather. If you don't know how dressy or casual your destination is, be as prepared as possible. Make a detailed list of everything you'll need, then set aside a place to assemble what you'll be packing.

Your contacts at the stores, appointments for fittings, delivery dates—keep track of them here. . . .

YOUR PICTURES

A word of caution: Don't plan on too many formal shots at the reception. They'll keep you from your guests.

YOUR BRIDAL PORTRAIT

No matter how informal the wedding itself, many brides want to have a formal portrait taken in their wedding gowns. If you're among this number, do some shopping around for a professional photographer who specializes in this kind of picture.

Make an appointment well in advance of the wedding to look at samples and discuss prices. This kind of photograph is not inexpensive, so you should consider all options very carefully.

Do you want your portrait in color or black and white? How many prints do you want? One for the groom? How many for each set of parents? Glossy prints for the newspapers?

Decide where the picture is to be taken. It may be in the photographer's studio, at your home, out of doors, or in the bridal shop.

The portrait session should take place several days before the wedding, especially if you want to use it along with the newspaper announcement—but make sure that your wedding dress and accessories will be ready.

Ask about makeup. And if you plan to have your hair done for the picture, let your hairdresser see your headpiece. (Let your sitting be a "dress rehearsal" for the wedding.)

Your formal portrait needn't be a stiff, impersonal photograph. There's no reason in the world why you can't have a more informal "formal"—especially if that's the tone you've set for the wedding. Why not have the photograph taken near the staircase in your living room? Or by a favorite tree in your backyard? Or schedule it for right after the ceremony so the groom can be included. Let your portrait reflect the way you feel about your wedding.

Remember—and this is important—to make firm financial arrangements about just what all the charges will be. (Note these on page 12.)

AT THE WEDDING AND RECEPTION

Your portrait photographer may also specialize in covering weddings: taking pictures of the bride dressing for the occasion, getting into or out of the car with her father, standing in the receiving line, cutting the wedding cake, et cetera. If he doesn't do this kind of work, or if you don't like his samples, arrange for another photographer to handle this end of the operation. Decide whether you want the pictures in color or in black and white. Then get a written statement detailing the cost of the photographs (with and without an album) and the price of each additional print and album. Give the photographer a list of the situations and people you want photographed. Give a duplicate list to a close friend, and ask her to check with the photographer from time to time. Explain the dos and don'ts of photographing inside the church. Be sure the photographer knows exactly where he is to be and when he is to be there.

THANK-YOU-CARD PICTURES

In some communities it is customary to wait until after the wedding to send out a small folder-type card that has a picture of the bride and groom, taken on the wedding day, inserted into or attached to it. Such cards have sufficient room for thank-you notes, and may be sent to anyone who gave a present, performed a favor, or provided valuable service.

AMATEUR HELPERS

Photography is such a popular hobby today that almost everyone knows somebody who takes excellent amateur candid shots. If you have such a gifted friend, why not ask him or her to bring a camera along and shoot at random. (You supply the film of course.)

YOUR FLOWERS

THE FLORIST

Select your florist carefully. The right one can contribute immeasurably to the success and smoothness of your wedding. Since satisfied customers are a florist's best recommendation, don't hesitate to ask around.

Consider your needs, then make your decisions accordingly. What do you have in mind for the ceremony and reception? What about bouquets and corsages? What color scheme do you have in mind? What are your favorite flowers? If your budget is limited, choose inexpensive in-season flowers, or use greens extensively and imaginatively. If you plan to do without the aid of a florist for the ceremony or the reception, make sure you place the task of selecting and arranging the flowers in capable hands.

AT THE CEREMONY

Often the only floral decorations are those on the altar, or at a Jewish wedding, the chupah. The church will undoubtedly have appropriate receptacles. If you wish, you may have the ends of some or all of the pews decorated with a few flowers or greens. Make your suggestions to the florist, but rely on his artistry and experience. Consult the clergyman too; he may have some helpful suggestions.

If you're being married at home or at a hotel or club, find an attractive spot for the ceremony—perhaps near a window or fireplace—and decide how flowers can enhance it.

AT THE RECEPTION

If you're having your reception at a club or hotel, floral decorations are usually included in the overall charge. Be sure to inquire.

If you want to handle this end of things yourself, consider what's in bloom in your own and your neighbors' gardens. Or use sprays of evergreens at Christmas time.

The buffet or bridal table should have a centerpiece or a twining of flat green leaves (any elaborate piece is likely to get in the way). You'll probably want flowers for other tables too—and don't forget a tiny blossom or two to be tied to the cake-cutting knife.

BOUQUETS AND CORSAGES

The bride's bouquet. Traditionally, this is white with touches of green. But if you prefer to carry a more colorful display, a single rose, or a basket of ivy, by all means do so.

Your attendants' bouquets. Here color is the main consideration. Show the florist a swatch of the dress fabric, and ask for his suggestions. Garlands for the hair, instead of headpieces, are a nice idea too. But not all hairstyles are suitable, so think twice.

Your going-away corsage. If you think a corsage will detract from your outfit, then dispense with this custom.

Corsages for mothers and grandmothers. These need not be identical; they are simply chosen to go with the colors of their dresses.

Boutonnieres for groom, best man, ushers, and both fathers. White carnations or roses are traditional, but you might want to consider a flower that's in your bouquet—even a colorful one.

DELIVERY

Give plenty of thought to when and where you want the flowers to be delivered. Give the florist a detailed list of names and addresses and times for delivery. And keep a copy. (If at all possible, it's a good idea to have all the bouquets, corsages, and boutonnieres delivered to the church.)

List your needs for the ceremony and the reception here....

29

TRANSPORTATION

Except at the smallest of informal weddings, where family, guests, and even the bridal party use their own cars to get where they're going, transportation must be a well-worked-out operation.

OUT-OF-TOWN GUESTS

Consider your out-of-town guests (and it's possible that your parents or your fiancé's parents are among the out-of-towners). They may have to be picked up at the airport, driven to parties, transported to the ceremony and then the reception, and finally taken back to where they are staying or to the airport. A good plan is to assign one friend or relative to each set of visitors, making him responsible for them throughout their stay.

TO AND FROM THE CEREMONY

At a large church wedding there are usually three chauffeur-driven cars: the first to carry the bride and her father to the church, the second for the bride's mother and a close relative or perhaps the maid of honor, the third for the groom and his best man. (If the bridesmaids are assembling at your home for pre-wedding photographs, there should be a fourth car for them.) These cars wait at the church and then drive to the reception, with the bride and groom in the first car, the bride's mother and father in the second, and the best man and maid of honor (or all the bridesmaids) in the third. Adjust this plan to meet your own needs. Whatever is practical, whatever will work, should be your guide.

If you'd like to use a limousine service, make your reservations fairly early in your planning. Their weekends are booked months in advance. Safe-driving friends with roomy cars can do the job nicely too.

Be sure each driver knows where he is to be, when he's to be there, and the names of the people he's to drive. Write out these instructions for each driver, including the addresses of the church and the place where the reception will be held.

If you want, you can arrange such transportation for the entire bridal party, the groom's family, and any special guests. Use the space at right to keep track of those you want to provide with transportation.

The bridal party should go directly from the ceremony to the place of the reception. There's no room for dawdling—especially if you're planning to allow enough time to freshen up and have additional formal photographs taken before the reception begins. Remember, the receiving line should be ready and waiting when your guests arrive.

Give some thought to the transportation scene after the reception too. If you plan to leave the reception in the groom's car, who will take care of getting it there? How will your parents get home? Who will see your attendants home? Will taxi service be available for guests who need it?

TRAFFIC AND PARKING

If the wedding will be sizable enough to present the possibility of creating a traffic jam either at the church or the reception, you should call the police and alert them to this potential problem. Most churches, clubs, and hotels have adequate parking space for a large number of cars, but if the ceremony or reception is to be at home, you may need to give the parking plans some extra attention. Can your guests find nearby parking places easily or should you hire someone to help direct them or even to park the cars for them?

PICKUPS AND DELIVERIES

For Out-of-Town Arrivals

Date	Person to be met	Place	Time	Address to be taken to	Person responsible

On the Wedding Day

Person to be picked up	Place	Time	Person responsible	Return to

YOUR WEDDING GIFTS

Share your wedding plans with your future mother-in-law. Take her shopping with you.
Call her. Keep her posted when you receive a gift from one of her friends.

Every wedding gift, large or small, is a token of someone's affection for you and your fiancé. And opening them is one of the pleasantest parts of getting married. There are those wonderful white elephants and those unexpected extravagances. And then there are those very special gifts that don't come in packages —the cheerful errand-running of your roommate, the skillful sewing of your aunt, the loving patience of your parents.

REGISTERING YOUR PREFERENCES

Surprise presents can be delightful, but there are undoubtedly a number of things you especially want or need. What better way to insure receiving exactly what you've set your heart on than to let friends know your wishes? And they'll appreciate having the choice made easier for them.

Make a list of what you want—not just silver and china but also appliances, linens, housewares, blankets—and record your preferences at the bridal registry of the store or stores that carry the items. Be sure to include a number of moderately priced things. Your mother and your maid of honor can steer friends to the appropriate stores. If your fiancé is from another city, his mother may want to have a list of your preferences for the stores in her town too.

Pick out your china, silver, and crystal patterns—with your fiancé, of course. Take time to consider them carefully—you'll be living with them all your life. If you're uncertain, postpone the decision. (One of your families may give you the money instead, to be invested when you're sure of your tastes.) *Note:* Check to see that the china and crystal you choose are "open stock" so you can order it by the piece. (Practically all silver is open stock.)

WHEN A WEDDING GIFT ARRIVES

Open the package carefully. Small parts of a gift can easily be thrown away with the wrappings. Look for the card; tape it to the present until you have a chance to record it. (No card? If the gift was sent from a store, call or write the store immediately. If not, does the postmark offer a clue?)

Record the gift as soon as possible. Use your card file (page 18) or the space on page 34.

If a gift arrives damaged, call or write the store at once. It's probably covered by insurance and can be replaced. If the present was home-wrapped and not insured, thank the donor, but don't mention the damage.

Save all warranties and instructions. These cards and pamphlets accompany most appliances and should be kept for future reference.

THANK-YOU NOTES

Start writing your thank-you notes as soon as the first gifts arrive. If you are away at school or not living in your hometown, ask someone on the home front to keep you posted as gifts are delivered.

Write on plain note paper or paper with the initials of your maiden name. Do not use paper with your married monogram until after the wedding (see page 25).

If a gift comes from a couple, address the thank-you note to the wife, but mention the husband in the body of your letter: "How very thoughtful of you and John to send us...."

If a gift comes from a group of people (say, twenty girls in your fiancé's office), you may write to them collectively. Address the note to the "head" person or the one you know best and ask her to thank the others. If, however, two or three friends send a present jointly, each should receive a note.

Write all notes yourself—and by hand. Printed or engraved acknowledgments or commercial thank-you cards are simply not as gracious as your own words.

DISPLAYING GIFTS

Displaying your presents for friends and relatives to admire is a pleasant, though completely optional, custom.

Where and when. If there is a relatively unused room in your house, that would be an ideal spot. It might be an unoccupied bedroom, alcove, or enclosed porch—anyplace that can be cleared of furniture and kept free for the period during which gifts are arriving. A week or so before the wedding, set up a long table or several card tables and cover them with floor-length white cloths. A few flowers or greens here and there add a nice touch. If your reception is to be at home, the gifts are often displayed at that time. If not, you may want to invite friends to drop in a few days before the wedding.

Arranging the gifts. In general, presents of the same type are placed together: silver in one spot, china in another, linens in still another. Don't put duplicates side by side unless they are something you would normally want to have in twos. Show just one place setting of silver, china, or crystal.

Displaying cards, to indicate who sent each gift, is a matter of personal choice. Showing them saves you from answering the inevitable "Who sent that?" Not showing them, on the other hand, saves comments and comparisons.

Displaying checks and gift certificates is another matter on which opinions differ. If you choose to show them, you may arrange them under glass, overlapping the checks so that the amounts are covered but the names visible. Or you may simply write on a white card: "Check from Aunt Joan and Uncle Ken."

Insuring your gifts. Although surely there is no danger that anyone invited to your house would make off with anything, many strangers will be making deliveries of one sort or another, and unless presents are kept locked up, someone might have an opportunity to steal them. Short-term insurance policies, called floaters, are available, and it might be wise to consider one of these to cover the period that gifts will be in the house—particularly the wedding day itself. Consult your insurance agent, or turn the task over to your father.

EXCHANGING GIFTS

This is a matter that calls for careful thought. You want to be certain no one's feelings will be hurt. If you plan to display your gifts, obviously nothing should be returned or exchanged before the wedding. After that, the most important consideration is whether the donor will ever know that his present has been replaced. If the gift is something that would not necessarily be seen when the giver visits you (a blanket, chafing dish, or kitchen appliance), it's probably safe to return it and choose something you want or need more. Or if a present comes from someone unlikely to call on you (a faraway relative or the president of your father's firm), chances are you are in no danger. Otherwise it is better to keep whatever was sent rather than risk offending someone who wished you well. Exception: An exact duplicate may be returned. Just be sure to remember *both* donors.

YOUR WEDDING YOUR WAY

What to do when you don't want wedding gifts sent to your parents' home? Maybe you're being married in the city where you work, many miles away from your hometown. The logistics of getting gifts opened, acknowledged, and then reshipped is something you'd like to do without. And you can—or at least you can minimize the problem. Word of mouth is the best way. The stores where you've registered can help out too. They'll mail the gifts any place you tell them to (you prepay, of course). Or they may arrange to notify you each time a gift is purchased (for your thank-you notes), store them for a few weeks, and then ship them to your new home all at one time.

Do a few thank-you notes every day so they won't pile up. Every gift should be acknowledged within a month.

YOUR GIFT RECORD

Name of Donor and Address	Gift and Store	Date Rec'd	Date Ack'd

YOUR PREWEDDING PARTIES

During the weeks and months that precede your wedding, no doubt a number of friends and relatives will want to entertain you and your fiancé. Indeed, dinner parties, cocktail parties, showers, and the like can be a delight. But too many can be tiring to everyone. So if the schedule seems to be getting overloaded and someone suggests entertaining you, thank her graciously and ask if you may have a raincheck for after the wedding trip.

If a prospective hostess should ask you to make up a list of people you want invited to a large party, do so promptly—with names, addresses, and telephone numbers. It's a good idea to add a note or two about your relationship to any guest your hostess doesn't know. Don't exceed the number of guests she suggests. And if she doesn't specify the size of the party, ask her.

SHOWERS

These may be given by anyone except a member of your or your fiancé's immediate family. Technically, the guest list for every shower should include all of your attendants who live nearby. But too many showers may put a burden on your roommate, while an out-of-town bridesmaid might feel hurt if not invited. Use your good sense in these matters.

If the hostess asks what kind of shower you would like, by all means express a preference: kitchen, linen, miscellaneous, whatever. Just be sure that you don't choose a category that calls for costly presents. Remember—many, if not all, of the guests will also be sending you wedding gifts.

Thank each giver as soon as you've opened the present. It's also nice—but not obligatory—to write a thank-you note. You should, however, write to the hostess, thanking her for the party; you should also acknowledge by letter any gifts sent by people who could not attend the party.

THE BRIDESMAIDS' DINNER

Here's a party you can host, and perhaps combine it with a display of your wedding presents. Or it may be given by a relative or by the attendants themselves. (This party is often held at the same time as the bachelor's dinner.) It provides a perfect opportunity to present your gifts to your bridesmaids—identical pieces of jewelry, key rings, or any similar permanent remembrance.

THE REHEARSAL, OR BRIDAL, DINNER

This is usually held immediately after the rehearsal. Often the groom's parents are hosts, but your family or even a close relative may do the honors. All the members of the wedding party (and their husbands or wives) and both sets of parents are always invited. The guest list may also include the clergyman (and his wife), out-of-town guests, and other friends.

Often it is a sit-down dinner, at home or at a hotel or club. It may be rather formal in character—with place cards, centerpieces, and wine for toasting—or it may be a simple, somewhat casual get-together. The type of wedding sets the tone. (If you plan to have the rehearsal dinner in your own home, look over the menus and recipes on pages 46-56 for some ideas. One of the do-ahead buffets might fit the bill perfectly.) Because of the hour, any children in the wedding party may be excluded—but it's nice to invite their parents instead.

Note: If your rehearsal dinner is scheduled for the night before the wedding, try to set it for an early hour. Everyone will want to get a good night's sleep.

THE REHEARSAL

Don't forget to plan your wedding music well ahead. Will it be organ, guitar, or dulcimer? A soloist or a group of singers? Note your thoughts here —for the prelude and processional, the ceremony, the recessional.

Unless yours is to be a civil ceremony or a small church wedding with only two attendants, it is really essential to have a rehearsal. Even if you are being married in your own home, you should run through the procedure at least once.

THE PROCEDURE

For a church wedding, timing is very important. The need for a system of signals soon becomes apparent. The clergyman, groom, and best man must appear on cue and not be left standing at the front of the church for minutes (which seem like eons to them) before the processional begins. The organist or musicians must know when to begin the processional music. And the bridesmaids and ushers should know where they should be standing when the bride reaches the altar. The clergyman can be a great help in determining the signals and procedures that work best in his church.

The rehearsal is often held the day before the wedding; but if all the attendants are in town, it could be two or three days in advance. Everyone involved in the ceremony should be present (and prompt): the clergyman, the organist or musicians, the participants, and the parents (though only the bride's father or whoever is giving her away is essential).

DECISIONS

This is the time to decide what step you will use in the processional. (Most people prefer a slow natural walk to the old hesitation step.)

The exact order of the processional, the grouping during the ceremony, and the order of the recessional must also be determined. The customs of different religions, denominations, and even churches vary so widely that it's best to let the clergyman take over here. But don't be shy with alternate suggestions. (The traditional orders are outlined at right.)

You must also settle the question of whether you take your father's right or left arm. Local customs differ, but it's really easier if you take his right arm. This way, after he has given you away, he does not have to cross in back of you to reach his seat beside your mother.

This is also the time to reaffirm that you and the clergyman agree on any variations in the ceremony itself. It might be a good idea to let him hear any special music you're planning to have, too. The more you deviate from the traditions, the more you should rehearse.

Be sure to check on anything you feel uncertain about.

Remind the ushers of any special seating arrangements; if they are at all complicated, give the head usher a list. If for any reason either the bride or groom's family is going to be scantily represented, instruct the ushers to seat guests equally on both sides.

Since all of the attendants will be a captive audience at this time, it's a good idea to review details: remind them when they are to be at the church, how they are to get there, where they are to wait...anything at all.

YOUR WEDDING YOUR WAY

An old superstition says that it's bad luck for the bride to rehearse her own wedding; rather, a substitute should play her part. But watching does not give you the same feeling of pace that you get by actually going through the motions. Our advice is to forget this old wives' tale and do your own rehearsing.

PROCESSIONAL

BRIDE   FATHER

FLOWER GIRL

RING-BEARER

MAID OF HONOR

BRIDESMAID   BRIDESMAID

BRIDESMAID   BRIDESMAID

USHER   USHER

USHER   USHER

USHER

BEST MAN GROOM

CLERGYMAN

ALTAR

Note: Bridesmaids may walk singly—especially if there are only two or three.

RECESSIONAL

ALTAR

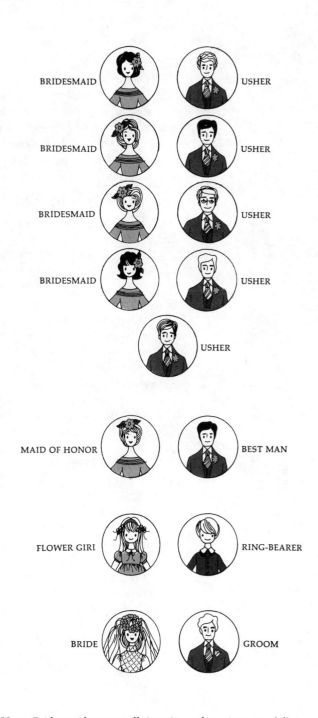

BRIDESMAID   USHER

BRIDESMAID   USHER

BRIDESMAID   USHER

BRIDESMAID   USHER

USHER

MAID OF HONOR   BEST MAN

FLOWER GIRI   RING-BEARER

BRIDE   GROOM

Note: Bridesmaids may walk in pairs; ushers, in pairs, follow.

THE CEREMONY

List your own countdown concerns here. . . .

The hour before the ceremony is the crucial one. That's when all the carefully planned elements come together. It's a good idea to provide a level-headed friend or relative—not a member of the wedding party—with a checklist of your last-minute concerns and ask her or him to check out each step.

THE FINAL COUNTDOWN

Here's the sequence for a traditional church wedding:

All flowers should have been delivered earlier in the day. If they have not arrived by at least an hour and a half before the ceremony, check with the florist.

All ushers should be at the church forty-five minutes to an hour ahead of time.

Music starts half an hour before the ceremony. (A soloist or choir does not sing until just before the processional.)

The bridesmaids arrive fifteen minutes to half an hour before the ceremony (unless they've dressed at the church). Be sure they know where they are to wait.

At about the same time, the groom and his best man arrive and go to the vestry.

The bride and her father are the last to arrive—(ten or fifteen minutes before the ceremony)—unless she has dressed at the church.

When the guests arrive, they are seated by the ushers, with relatives and honored friends being seated in the front pews. The head usher should have a list of these special guests.

Just before the processional is to begin, the groom's mother is escorted by the head usher (or an usher in her family) to the front pew on the right. The groom's father follows directly behind them. The head usher then escorts the bride's mother to the front pew on the left. (If the bride's brother is an usher, he would escort his mother.) After this, no other guests are ushered down the aisle.

At a formal wedding, two ushers stretch aisle ribbons and unroll the aisle carpet.

The processional music starts, and the bride's mother rises as a signal for the guests to stand. The clergyman, followed by the groom and best man, steps to the altar, and the processional begins.

SPECIAL CIRCUMSTANCES

At an informal home or garden wedding, the bride and groom may mingle with the guests before the ceremony. When the ceremony is about to begin, everyone simply takes his or her place.

At a second wedding, the same is often true. If the ceremony is in a church or chapel, the bride and groom may come directly from the vestry. (A bride is not given away twice.) There are usually just two attendants. If the bride's first marriage was of very short duration and if that ceremony was very low-key (an elopement), the bride may opt for all the traditions of a church wedding.

At a double wedding, the father may walk between the brides (sisters) if they share attendants. Or the younger bride, escorted by a male relative (or her own father), would follow the elder. If there are two sets of attendants, all the ushers walk together. They are followed by the elder bride's attendants, the elder bride, the younger bride's attendants, and the younger bride. The younger bride follows the elder in the recessional.

The seating of divorced parents. Divorced parents do not sit together. The mother (either bride's or groom's) sits in the front pew (with her husband if she has remarried); the father (with his present wife if any) sits in the third.

YOUR RECEPTION

When the wedding ceremony is over, you and your company move on to the reception. Whether this means a drive of several miles or a short walk from one room to another, arrange for a brief respite between events—to catch your breath, touch up your makeup, or let the photographer take a picture or two.

TYPES OF RECEPTIONS

For the most part, your reception echoes the tone of your wedding. If the ceremony is a formal gathering with a great many guests and a large bridal party, the reception will probably be a rather elaborate affair. If the wedding has been less formal, some of the reception rituals and embellishments may be omitted. (Simply choose the ones that appeal to you and ignore the others.) And if the wedding was informal, the reception becomes a party of whatever sort you like.

An ultra-formal reception always begins with a receiving line (see the diagram on page 41). There is almost always champagne, as well as a selection of other drinks. A full formal meal, an elaborate buffet, or a wide selection of hors d'oeuvres is served. If it is a full meal, it is served by waiters, and the guests are seated at tables marked with place cards. There are also a bridal table and a parents' table (see diagrams on page 41), extensive decorations, a multitiered cake, an orchestra (large or small), and dancing.

A formal reception is similar but less elaborate. Often the two fathers do not stand in the receiving line. There will be a meal or hors d'oeuvres, champagne, and cake. Usually there is a bridal table but the parents' table is optional. There may be place cards for a sit-down meal; at a buffet guests serve themselves and sit wherever they like. More often than not there is some kind of music, possibly a small orchestra or trio, for dancing.

An informal reception follows few rules. If you dispense with the receiving line, you and your new husband should stand near the entrance of the room to greet the guests. Refreshments may be no more than wine and a wedding cake, or a full-course meal may be served. Although dancing is optional, you will probably want to have background music, perhaps from a talented friend who plays the piano or guitar.

An at-home reception may be any degree of formality, depending on the kind of wedding that precedes it and on the size of the home. Large or small, ultra-formal or informal, it calls for extra planning. Does excess furniture have to be moved? Does additional furniture have to be rented? Where will the receiving line stand? Do you need extra glasses,

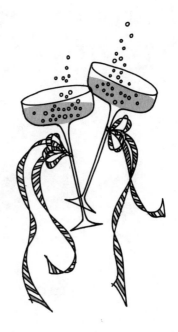

YOUR WEDDING YOUR WAY

If a traditional reception, formal or informal, doesn't appeal to you, plan a party that does. And it can even take place weeks after the ceremony. Consider having a huge cocktail party in your new, sparsely furnished apartment. Or treat a few close friends to a weekend at a ski lodge. Choose a lakeside spot or wooded glen and serve a French *pique-nique* in individual wicker baskets. Reserve a private dining room in a Slavic restaurant and dance to gypsy music. However you choose to celebrate the occasion, you should be happy and gay in the way you like best.

dishes, and silver? What about ashtrays and ice? Who will answer the door, take the coats, cover the telephone? How and where will the food be served, the cake cut, the wine poured? Do you have enough help? Will there be room for dancing? Where will the musicians be? If you're planning an outdoor reception, do you have an alternate plan in case of rain? Can you rent a tent or awning?

Many caterers specialize in wedding receptions, and if you work closely with them, they can provide all the help you need—from setting up the physical arrangements in the house or garden to preparing and serving the meal to cleaning up afterward. But choose your caterer carefully, preferably on the recommendation of someone he has served recently. Discuss your needs and wishes well in advance of the wedding day; be sure to get all estimates in writing. Find out who will be in charge during the reception.

Maybe you'd like to handle the reception yourself. Family and friends can pitch in with the food preparation if you wish. And buffet tables simplify the serving set-up. Even so, consider hiring one or two people to help out. Look over the menus and recipes on pages 46-63—you'll find reception plans that will adapt nicely to almost any type of party and any size guest list.

THE RECEIVING LINE

The purpose of a receiving line is obvious. It provides an easy, systematic way for the friends and relatives of both families to greet the new bride and groom and to wish them well.

Who receives? The receiving line may consist of all the people indicated in the diagram at right or it may be abbreviated, to include only the mother of the bride, the mother of the groom, the bride, the groom, and the maid of honor.

Either or both of the fathers may receive if they like, or they may simply mingle with guests. Often the groom's father stands in the receiving line (particularly if most of the guests are strangers to him), while the bride's father forgoes the line and sees to his duties as host.

The best man and ushers never stand in the receiving line. Instead, they make themselves generally available and helpful to other guests.

Child attendants seldom stand in the line—they tend to become restless all too quickly.

What do you say? The bride's mother greets each guest, shakes hands, and introduces him to the groom's father (or mother if the father is not receiving). If a guest does not know the bride's mother, he is expected to volunteer his name and explain his connection: "I'm Frank Sherwood. Matthew and I work together." The groom's father merely says, "How do you do," or some approximation thereof, and introduces the guest to his wife. And so on down the line. As the bride, you will probably know most of the guests and will want to say something personal to many of them—thanking them for their gifts or for coming a long distance or perhaps asking about a member of their family. Unless the guest list is small, however, it's a good idea to keep conversation to a few brief remarks so that other guests are not kept waiting in line. Occasionally a name becomes a bit distorted as it gets repeated down the line. If you didn't catch the name of a stranger, you may ask him to repeat it, or you may simply say, "I'm so glad you could come." (It's a fair assumption that if you don't know the guest, he is a friend of the groom's family.)

A bridesmaid is usually introduced by her full name: "Linda Godfrey" rather than "Miss Godfrey."

Special situations. Family circumstances often require adjustments in the standard setup for the receiving line as follows:

If your mother is not living, your father stands at the beginning of the line.

If your parents are divorced and your mother gives the reception, she stands alone in the receiving line. Your stepfather acts as host. Your real father (and your stepmother), if they attend, are guests; they do not stand in the receiving line.

If your parents are divorced and your father gives the reception (which is often the case when a divorced mother has sponsored the wedding), he stands first in line. If he has remarried, he would be followed in the receiving

RECEIVING LINE

BRIDE'S MOTHER · GROOM'S FATHER · GROOM'S MOTHER · BRIDE'S FATHER · BRIDE · GROOM · MAID OF HONOR · BRIDESMAIDS

Note: Bridesmaids stand in the order in which they walked in the processional, with the girl who led the procession at the end of the line.

BRIDAL TABLE

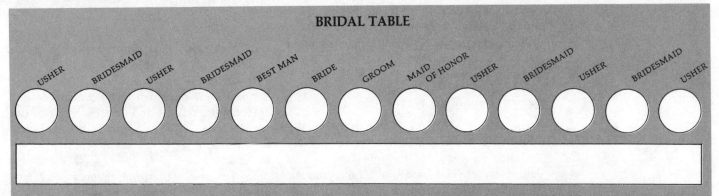

USHER · BRIDESMAID · USHER · BRIDESMAID · BEST MAN · BRIDE · GROOM · MAID OF HONOR · USHER · BRIDESMAID · USHER · BRIDESMAID · USHER

Note: This is usually a long table, often on a platform, with all members of the bridal party (except children). Everyone faces the rest of the room, as at a speaker's table. Often the clergyman or a close friend who could not be in the wedding party is included.

PARENTS' TABLE

Note: If the table is large enough, other honored guests (such as grandparents, sisters, and brothers) are seated at the parents' table, alternating men and women. Child attendants might also sit here. At a small wedding, the parents might sit at the bridal table.

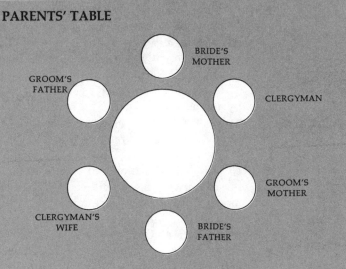

BRIDE'S MOTHER · GROOM'S FATHER · CLERGYMAN · CLERGYMAN'S WIFE · GROOM'S MOTHER · BRIDE'S FATHER

line by your stepmother. Your mother (and stepfather) would then attend the reception as guests... or not at all.

If relations between divorced parents are friendly, your mother may stand next to your father, in which case your father's wife would circulate among the guests, playing the role of hostess.

If the groom's parents are divorced, only his mother stands in the receiving line.

How long do you receive? The receiving line should not disband until every guest has been greeted. If the gathering is large, it may take half an hour or longer, and everyone should remain standing and smiling to the end. It is assumed, however, that all guests will arrive promptly and go through the line immediately; so if anyone is late or stops to talk to other guests before going through the line, it is not necessary to wait for him.

THE FEAST

The type of refreshments you serve will depend on the time of day and on the atmosphere you want to create for the reception. If you plan to handle the food and drink yourself (with the aid of friends or some hired help), you will find a number of menu and recipe ideas on pages 45-63.

A reception following a morning wedding (which includes a noon ceremony) is called a wedding breakfast, even though the food may be rather elegant luncheon fare. There is usually a first course, a hot entrée, rolls, salad, and ice cream to go with the cake. Service may be at tables or buffet style.

An afternoon wedding is generally followed by a stand-up reception. This may be as simple as cake and champagne or it may include sandwiches and cocktail party fare.

An early evening wedding (five or six o'clock) calls for a dinner of some sort, usually served between seven and eight. The seating may be formal, with place cards, or it may be buffet style, with guests seating themselves. In either case, a full dinner is served.

An evening wedding (seven to nine o'clock) is followed by a supper which is simpler than dinner and usually served buffet style.

THE DRINKS

There was a time when certain religious, ethnic, and regional groups took a strong stand against any sort of alcoholic drink. But today most people like to—and even expect to—celebrate a wedding with something stronger than fruit punch. At a formal reception there is always champagne (imported or domestic) for toasting, and there is also bar service. The same plan may hold true for smaller, more informal receptions, or the choice may be limited to champagne or a wine punch only. Whatever your plans, it is only thoughtful to provide a nonalcoholic punch or soft drinks for those who prefer them.

Certainly drinks do add greatly to the festivity of the occasion, but they can also turn out to be your most unpredictable expense. Unless money is no object, it's wise to set some sort of limit in advance. If the reception is at home, simply order what you consider to be a reasonable amount—and an extra bottle or two for a reserve. You can figure on about twenty-five drinks (one ounce each) from each fifth of liquor and eight servings (three ounces each) from each bottle of champagne. If you are dealing with a caterer, he will usually supply enough to last as long as you like, charging you only for the number of bottles opened. Someone (probably your father) should instruct him to serve until either a certain number of bottles have been consumed or a certain hour arrives. When either of these points has been reached, the caterer informs your father, who may decide that he wants to extend the original estimate or that it's time to begin closing the bar.

TOASTS

When the bridal party has been seated at the bridal table (or if there is no bridal table, when the receiving line has broken up), the champagne glasses are filled and passed, the orchestra (if there is one) signals for attention, and the best man rises to propose a toast to the bride and groom. All of the guests also rise and drink. (The bride and groom remain seated and do not drink.) This may be the only toast or it may be one of many, depending on how many

If you're having a sit-down dinner, plan your table groupings well in advance. Who will enjoy who's company? Use place cards or assign each guest to a specific table.

outgoing friends and relatives are in attendance. Sometime shortly after the initial toast, the best man reads aloud any telegrams sent by people who cannot be present.

MUSIC AND DANCING

Dancing is optional at all but the most formal receptions. And because it calls for a fairly large area, uncarpeted and cleared of all furniture, it is often omitted at a more informal reception.

When there is dancing, the orchestra should be ready to start playing when the first guests arrive at the reception. Background music may be played until the receiving line has broken up. Or at a large affair guests may be encouraged to dance as soon as they have gone through the line. When the wedding party is assembled at the bridal table, the orchestra plays a fanfare to clear the floor and bring guests to attention; it is then silent while the toast or toasts are proposed (see page 42).

When the toasts are completed and any telegrams have been read, the sequence of the wedding dance begins. The bride and groom dance the first dance together, circling the floor alone. Then the bride's father cuts in on her, and the groom dances with the bride's mother. After a minute or so the groom's father dances with the bride and the groom dances with his mother while the bride's parents dance together. Then everyone joins in.

At a sit-down reception, further dancing may be postponed until the meal is over or it may continue between courses.

During the course of the reception, the best man and each usher should dance with the bride, the maid of honor, and each bridesmaid.

The music may consist of popular current songs or old favorites. You may leave the choice to the orchestra, or you may prefer to supply them with a list of special requests. If you and your new husband have a favorite song, by all means ask that it be played. Or if there is a strong ethnic strain in either or both families—Irish, for example—request some well-known airs. You may want to ask the orchestra leader to dedicate certain numbers to beloved relatives or other guests.

The rules for reception music, whether for dancing or background, are highly elastic, and most orchestra leaders and musicians are happy to oblige with any tune they know. You and your guests may request whatever you like as long as it is not raucous.

THE CAKE

Whatever else is served at the reception, you'll surely want a wedding cake. It may be home baked (see the recipes on pages 57-61), bought at a bakery, or furnished by the caterer. It may be one tier or several (three is average), of almost any flavor (a light-colored cake is traditional), frosted and decorated any way you like—within reason.

The groom's cake—usually a fruitcake—may form the top tier of the wedding cake, or it may be a separate cake cut and boxed for guests to take home (see page 60).

Cutting the cake. About an hour before they leave the reception to change their clothes, the bride and groom cut the cake with a silver knife, usually decorated with a few flowers tied to the handle with a ribbon. The groom places his right hand over the bride's and together they cut the first slice from the bottom tier, divide it, and eat it. Then someone else takes over the cutting and serving chores. (At a simple afternoon reception, the cake-cutting takes place much earlier.)

THE GUEST BOOK

Entirely optional, but a delightful memento of the happy day, is an attractively bound guest book in which everyone signs his name. These books are available at many jewelry stores, stationery departments, and bridal shops. You may station a friend at the end of the receiving line to ask the guests to sign, or you may ask the best man or maid of honor to circulate among the guests to make sure everyone's signature is included.

TOSSING THE BOUQUET

Your reception may last one hour or several, but it should be long enough to enjoy any traditional rituals you wish to include, to enjoy your food and wine, and to move around

among your guests, stopping for a few moments at each table or with each group. When you are ready to change into your going-away clothes, it's time to throw your bouquet. (If a corsage is part of the bouquet, remove it first and give it to the maid of honor for safekeeping.) The orchestra may play another musical signal, or the maid of honor may simply spread the word around. Then all unmarried girls gather around you. According to tradition, you are supposed to turn your back and throw the bouquet over your shoulder at random; superstition has it that the girl who catches it will be the next bride. Most girls today face forward, however, and as a gesture of affection throw their bouquets to someone special.

In many communities the tossing of the bridal bouquet is followed by the tossing of the bride's garter, with the groom throwing the garter out to the assembled unmarried men.

SAYING GOOD-BYE

When the bouquet has been thrown, you and your maid of honor go immediately to the room where you plan to dress. (Because she still has responsibilities as hostess, your mother does not come with you at this time.) This is the time to remind your maid of honor to take care of any loose ends, such as making sure your wedding gown gets home safely, seeing to it that the groom's cake gets distributed or taken home to be frozen, or tending to any detail that concerns you.

If the groom is formally dressed, he leaves to change at the same time. If he is already wearing a business suit, he can use the time to check with the best man and make sure that all last minute details concerning your departure and wedding trip have been taken care of.

When you are both dressed and ready to go, there is a final, very important moment when each of you privately says good-bye and thank you to your own parents. This should be a warm but brief interlude. You will all be feeling strong emotions, and often a hug and a kiss says everything best. But do be sure to have a little time alone with your parents.

Meanwhile the best man is in charge, making sure that the car is at the door, that the suitcases are accounted for, and that tickets, hotel reservations, and the like are ready to be handed to the groom. And finally you and your new husband make your departure amid good-byes, good wishes . . . and a shower of rice or paper petals.

HOW LONG DOES A RECEPTION LAST?

This depends on many factors: the advance arrangements you have made, how far you are traveling after the reception, and very practically, your budget. If the reception is held at an establishment that regularly caters such affairs, you will have engaged the rooms for a certain number of hours at a certain fee. And since there may well be another party scheduled for the same rooms a bit later, the management will insist upon guests leaving promptly. If the reception is at a club or hotel, the staff may be willing to let it go on as long as you like. But remember that every additional hour will cost extra if the orchestra continues to play and that every additional round of drinks will increase the bar bill substantially. So even if no one is pressing you, it's a good idea to stick to your original time schedule for making your departure, for this is the signal to guests that the party is over.

BACK-TO-THE-HOUSE PARTIES

If the reception is held relatively early in the day, it is becoming increasingly common for the bride's parents to invite a few special friends to go back home with them afterward for an informal postscript party. (If the reception is held at home, a small group may be asked to stay on.) The groom's parents may attend this party, or they may ask their friends back to their house if they live nearby or to their hotel if they are from out of town. Unless guests are specifically asked to linger, they should leave the reception soon after the bride and groom depart.

If both sets of parents are from out of town (which is often the case these days), it's a nice idea to ask a roommate or close friend to entertain them after the reception—or perhaps even more thoughtfully, the day after—as a pleasant wind-up to the wedding festivities.

A nice thought: Call or wire both sets of parents the day after the wedding to thank them for everything.

MENUS & RECIPES

Although a professionally catered reception can be very impressive, there is something uniquely warm and charming about a wedding celebration prepared by you and the people closest to you. And it somehow seems all the more special when it takes place at home or in the social room of the church you've attended since earliest Sunday school days.

The reception can be any size—depending on your budget, the physical space, and an honest assessment of just how much you can handle. But whether the party is large or small, the menu itself must be carefully and realistically planned. A good rule of thumb: The larger the gathering, the simpler the menu. You and one or two willing recruits can undoubtedly prepare a sit-down meal for twelve. But if you plan to have more than a hundred people share in the merry-making, you'd better confine yourself to a sparkling jewel-colored punch, a beautiful wedding cake, and heaping dishes of candies and nuts.

The important difference between a do-it-yourself party and a let-Monsieur-Georges-do-it catered affair is that all the advance strategy and detailed delegation of duties falls squarely on your shoulders.

Begin your tactical planning with two known factors: the number of guests and the kitchen and serving facilities available. Then choose whatever party foods can be served easily and gracefully within these boundaries. Next, line up your volunteer helpers and assign very specific jobs to each. If someone is going to be making and decorating the cake, be sure that you both understand exactly when and how it is going to be delivered. (If you plan to bake the cake yourself, do as much as you can in advance—see page 62.) If casseroles or relishes are arriving early in the day, make

certain that refrigerator shelves have been cleared to accommodate them. When members of a church guild are doing the honors, they probably know the routines very well, so consult them about delivery times and other arrangements. Be sure, too, that they understand exactly how you want the food to be heated, the tables set up, the platters garnished, and so forth.

Now, make a down-to-the-last-pickle-fork list of everything needed for serving and eating. You may want to rent part or all of this equipment. Punch bowls, cups, flat silver, serving dishes, glasses, flower vases, and ashtrays are all available from catering supply firms. And while you're thinking about it, consider engaging a couple of people to handle the actual serving. Even though your family and friends are happy to do all the groundwork, once the party begins they should be free to enjoy it, not busy in the kitchen or occupied refilling glasses or passing trays. And this applies doubly to you. Do as much as you like and can manage before the wedding. But don't, under any circumstances, plan to don an apron for your own reception.

On the following pages are four complete menus—complete with wedding cakes—for four quite different kinds of receptions. Follow them to the letter, if you like—all are precision tested for smooth performance. Or, if you prefer, simply make them a point of departure for your own preferential planning. Adapt them for a prewedding party, if that's what you have in mind (all it takes is a simple switch of desserts). Or use the cake from one menu with the punch from another. Choose with your own color theme in mind. After all, your feast, like everything else about this very special day, is part of your wedding your way.

A WEDDING BREAKFAST FOR 12

Strawberries in Champagne or
Mulled Tomato Juice

Oven Omelet Squares with Canadian Bacon

Cranberry Relish Ring

Brioches   Tea Ring

Butter Balls and Butter Curls

Petits Fours Wedding Cake (page 61)
or Danish Puff

Coffee   Tea

There's something special, a little bit out of the ordinary, about an intimate breakfast after a small morning wedding. And here's a delightfully different menu that will fill the bill in a most attractive way. What's more, most of the food can be made well ahead of time. The Brioches and/or Tea Ring can be baked weeks in advance and then frozen. The molded relish ring is a day-before assignment. Even the tomato juice and the omelet can be mixed the night before and refrigerated. The simple schedule for after the ceremony: Unmold the salad, pop the omelet into the oven, reheat the Brioches (right along with the omelet), and plug in the percolator.

Buffet service is in order here. Arrange the food on the dining-room table; guests serve themselves and move to little tables or trays in the living room, or even outdoors. Or you can set out the buffet on a sideboard and let everyone sit together at the preset table.

This menu will come in handy for any number of prewedding occasions—when the prospective in-laws get together for the first time, when friends come to look at your gifts, when the out-of-town members of the wedding party converge. (In any of these instances, substitute the Danish Puff for the cake.)

STRAWBERRIES IN CHAMPAGNE

1 quart fresh small strawberries
2 bottles (⅘ quart each) champagne,
   chilled

Place 2 or 3 strawberries (hulled or unhulled) in each stemmed glass; fill glasses with champagne.   *12 servings (about 4 ounces each).*

MULLED TOMATO JUICE

2 cans (46 ounces each) tomato juice
1 tablespoon Worcestershire sauce
1 teaspoon salt
1 teaspoon celery salt
½ teaspoon oregano
5 drops red pepper sauce
½ cup soft butter

Measure all ingredients into 15-cup automatic percolator (with basket removed). Let it perk one cycle. Arrange small mugs around the percolator and then let your guests serve themselves.   *15 servings (about ¾ cup each).*

OVEN OMELET SQUARES WITH CANADIAN BACON

¼ cup butter or margarine
1½ dozen eggs
1 cup dairy sour cream
1 cup milk
2 teaspoons salt
¼ cup chopped green onions
1 pound Canadian-style bacon,
   cut into 24 slices
¼ cup maple-flavored syrup

Heat oven to 325°. In oven, melt butter in baking dish, 13½x9x2 inches. Tilt dish to coat bottom with butter. In large mixer bowl, beat eggs, sour cream, milk, and salt until blended. Stir in onions. Pour into baking dish.

Reassemble slices of bacon on aluminum foil. Pour syrup over roll. Wrap and place in baking pan.

Place baking dish and baking pan in oven. Bake until eggs are set but still moist and bacon is hot, about 35 minutes.

Cut omelet into twelve 3-inch squares. Arrange on warm platter with bacon slices and garnish with parsley.   *12 servings.*

CRANBERRY RELISH RING

2 cups boiling water
2 packages (3 ounces each) orange-
  flavored gelatin
2 packages (10 ounces each) frozen
  cranberry-orange relish
1 can (13½ ounces) crushed pineapple
½ cup chopped walnuts
  Salad greens
  Small bunches seedless green grapes

Pour boiling water over gelatin in large bowl; stir until gelatin is dissolved. Add frozen relish, pineapple (with syrup), and walnuts; stir until relish is thawed. Pour into 6-cup ring mold. Refrigerate until firm, at least 12 hours.

Unmold onto salad greens on serving plate. Fill center of salad with bunches of green grapes.   *12 servings.*

PARTY BUTTER PATS

Butter Balls: Scald a pair of wooden butter paddles in boiling water 30 seconds; chill in ice and water. Cut ¼-pound stick of firm butter into 1-inch squares. Cut each square in half; stand each half upright on paddle. Smack butter between paddles. Hold bottom paddle still and rotate top paddle to form ball. If butter clings to paddles, dip them again into hot water, then into ice and water. Drop finished balls into bowl of ice and water; cover and refrigerate. Dip paddles into ice and water before making each ball. One ¼-pound stick of butter will make 8 to 10 butter balls.

Butter Curls: Let butter curler stand in hot water at least 10 minutes. Pull curler firmly across surface of ¼-pound stick of firm butter. (Butter should not be too cold or curls will break.) Drop curls into bowl of ice and water; cover and refrigerate. Dip curler into hot water before making each curl. One ¼-pound stick of butter will make about 12 butter curls.

BRIOCHES

So rich, so continental. Make them ahead of time; heat them right along with the omelet.

1 package active dry yeast
¾ cup warm water (105 to 115°)
½ cup sugar
½ teaspoon salt
3 eggs
1 egg yolk (reserve white)
½ cup butter or margarine, softened
3½ cups all-purpose flour*
1 tablespoon sugar

In large mixer bowl, dissolve yeast in warm water. Add ½ cup sugar, the salt, eggs, egg yolk, butter, and 2 cups of the flour. Blend on low speed ½ minute, scraping bowl constantly. Beat on medium speed 10 minutes, scraping bowl occasionally. Stir in remaining flour until smooth. Scrape batter from side of bowl. Cover; let rise in warm place until double, about 1 hour.

Stir down batter by beating 25 strokes. Cover tightly; refrigerate at least 8 hours. (At this point, dough can be refrigerated up to 2 days.)

Stir down batter. Divide dough in half; place one half on lightly floured surface (keep other half chilled). Shape dough into roll, about 8 inches long. Cut into 16 pieces.

Shape 12 pieces into balls and place in greased medium muffin cups. (Work very quickly with floured hands as dough is soft and sticky.) Flatten and make a deep indentation in center of each ball. Cut each of the remaining 4 pieces into 3 equal parts. Shape each part into a small ball; place ball in each indentation. Repeat with other half of dough. Let rise until double, about 40 minutes.

Heat oven to 375°. Beat reserved egg white and 1 tablespoon sugar slightly; brush on rolls. Bake 15 to 20 minutes.   *24 rolls.*

*If using self-rising flour, omit salt.

TO FREEZE: Cool completely, wrap in aluminum foil, and freeze. (Do not freeze longer than 9 months.) To thaw, heat foil-wrapped Brioches in 325° oven about 30 minutes or leave at room temperature 2 to 3 hours.

Remember to make out a detailed shopping list— right down to the salt and pepper.

TEA RING

This coffee cake has great style—it's elegant and earthy. The handsome ring, with its surprising blend of colors and flavors in the filling, may prove to be the conversation piece of your party.

      1 package active dry yeast
    ¼ cup warm water (105 to 115°)
    ¼ cup lukewarm milk (scalded
         then cooled)
    ¼ cup sugar
    ½ teaspoon salt
      1 egg
    ¼ cup shortening, butter, or margarine,
         softened
 2¼ to 2½ cups all-purpose flour*
         Apricot-Cherry Filling (below)
         Glaze (right)

In large mixing bowl, dissolve yeast in warm water. Stir in milk, sugar, salt, egg, shortening, and half the flour. Beat until smooth. Mix in enough remaining flour to make dough easy to handle.

Turn dough onto lightly floured board; knead until smooth and elastic, about 5 minutes. Place in greased bowl; turn greased side up. (At this point, dough can be covered and refrigerated up to 4 days.) Cover; let rise in warm place until double, about 1½ hours. Dough is ready if impression remains when touched.

Punch down dough. Roll into rectangle, 15x9 inches. Spread Apricot-Cherry Filling on rectangle. Roll up, beginning at wide side. Pinch edge of dough into roll to seal well. Stretch roll to make even.

Shape into ring with sealed edge down on lightly greased baking sheet. Pinch ends together. With scissors, make cuts ⅔ of the way through ring at 1-inch intervals. Turn each section on its side. Cover; let rise until double, about 30 minutes.

Heat oven to 375°. Bake 25 to 30 minutes. Cool 1 hour; drizzle with Glaze. *12 servings.*

Apricot-Cherry Filling: Mix ½ cup finely chopped dried apricots and ½ cup drained finely chopped maraschino cherries.

Glaze: Blend 2 cups confectioners' sugar, ¼ cup butter, softened, 1 teaspoon vanilla, and about 2 tablespoons water.

*If using self-rising flour, omit salt.

TO FREEZE: Freeze baked ring (unglazed) uncovered 2 hours. Wrap in aluminum foil and return to freezer. (Do not freeze longer than 9 months.) To thaw, heat foil-wrapped ring in 325° oven about 35 minutes or leave at room temperature 2 to 3 hours. When cool, glaze.

DANISH PUFF

Here's a delicious cross between a dessert and a coffee cake. To be on the safe side, make the recipe twice and count on two servings for each guest.

    ½ cup butter or margarine, softened
      1 cup all-purpose flour*
      2 tablespoons water
    ½ cup butter or margarine
      1 cup water
      1 teaspoon almond extract
      1 cup all-purpose flour*
      3 eggs
         Confectioners' Sugar Glaze (below)
         Chopped nuts

Heat oven to 350°. Cut ½ cup butter into 1 cup flour. Sprinkle with 2 tablespoons water; mix. Round into ball; divide in half. Pat each half into strip, 12x3 inches, on ungreased baking sheet. Strips should be about 3 inches apart.

In medium saucepan, heat ½ cup butter and 1 cup water to rolling boil. Remove from heat; quickly stir in almond extract and 1 cup flour. Stir vigorously over low heat until mixture forms a ball, about 1 minute. Remove from heat. Add eggs all at once; beat until smooth and glossy. Divide in half; spread each half evenly over strips. Bake until topping is crisp and brown, about 60 minutes. Cool. Frost with Confectioners' Sugar Glaze and sprinkle generously with nuts.   *12 servings.*

*Self-rising flour can be used in this recipe.

Confectioners' Sugar Glaze: Mix 1½ cups confectioners' sugar, 2 tablespoons butter or margarine, softened, 1½ teaspoons vanilla, and 1 to 2 tablespoons warm water until smooth.

A BUFFET FOR 24

Daiquiri Punch

Beef Stroganoff with Rice

Green Salad Provençe

Relish Trays (page 52)

Tiny Hot Rolls (page 53)

Twin Ice-cream Bombes

Twin Hearts Wedding Cake (page 57)

Coffee   Tea

Think you can't handle a dinner reception yourself? Think again! The look is dramatic but the preparation is relatively easy. The key is planning. Just about everything can be put together (at least partially) in advance. The rolls and ice-cream bombes can be made well ahead and stored in the freezer. (The cake layers too can be baked and then frozen.) The stroganoff, salad greens, and relishes call for day-before attention. Your main concern for the reception, then, will be getting the food onto the table. And here you'll have to rely on friends or any help you've hired for the occasion. (It's a good idea to write out special instructions, with reheating hints and notes about which serving dishes to use.) The stroganoff is ideal for chafing dish service, and the rice can go right from oven to table if your casseroles are attractive.

A need-no-knife meal like this is perfect for buffet service. Guests can serve themselves from the sideboard or dining-room table and then move on to another room.

We like the versatility of the menu plan, too. Just think about the possibilities—for a "meet my fiancé" party, an after-the-rehearsal dinner, or a late supper *after* the wedding reception (with the ice-cream bombes instead of the cake).

DAIQUIRI PUNCH

1 bottle (⅘ quart) white rum, chilled
1¼ cups (12 ounces) bottled daiquiri mix, chilled
2 quarts carbonated lemon-lime beverage, chilled

Pour rum and daiquiri mix into large punch bowl; stir in carbonated beverage. Serve immediately. Garnish with an Ice Ring (below) or arrange a garland of flowers and green leaves around the bowl.   *25 servings (about ½ cup each).*

NOTE: Depending on the size of the gathering—and whether you're serving champagne and other drinks—you can make this punch in larger quantities (see chart below). But don't overdo. It might be wiser to fill in with freshly made "seconds" and "thirds" for a small group.

SERVINGS (ABOUT ½ CUP)

	50	75	100
White Rum	2 bottles	3 bottles	4 bottles
Daiquiri Mix	2½ cups	3¾ cups	5 cups
Lemon-Lime Beverage	4 quarts	6 quarts	8 quarts

ICE RINGS

Arrange thin overlapping slices of lime, orange, and lemon in a ring mold. (Make sure the ring mold fits into the punch bowl you'll be using.) Pour water into mold to partially cover fruit (about ¼ inch); freeze. When frozen, add more water to fill mold ¾ full; freeze. Unmold ring and float fruit side up in punch. For a crystal-clear ice ring, boil and cool the water before pouring into mold.

For a more colorful ring, add about ⅓ cup cranberries with the fruit slices or alternate fruit slices and whole strawberries in the mold.

Carnations, roses, mums, or other flowers can be frozen in an ice ring too. Wash flowers, remove stems, and place blossom side down in mold.

BEEF STROGANOFF WITH RICE

6 pounds beef sirloin steak,
   ¾ inch thick
¾ cup butter or margarine
3 cans (6 ounces each) sliced
   mushrooms, drained
6 cans (10½ ounces each) condensed
   beef broth (bouillon)
1 cup instant minced onion
¾ cup catsup
1 tablespoon plus 1½ teaspoons
   garlic salt
1 cup all-purpose flour
   Easy Oven Rice (below)
1½ quarts dairy sour cream (6 cups)

Trim fat and bone from meat; cut meat into strips, 3x¼ inch. Melt butter in large Dutch oven or roasting pan. Add mushrooms; cook and stir about 5 minutes. Remove mushrooms. Cook meat in same pan until light brown. Reserve 2 cups of the broth; stir remaining broth, the onion, catsup, and garlic salt into Dutch oven. Cover and simmer 15 minutes.

Mix reserved broth and the flour; stir into meat mixture. Stir in mushrooms; heat to boiling, stirring constantly. Boil and stir 1 minute. Cool; cover and refrigerate.

About 45 minutes before serving, prepare rice. Heat stroganoff over low heat. Stir in sour cream; heat just until hot. Serve on rice. *24 servings (about ¾ cup meat mixture and ¾ cup rice).*

NOTE: The meat mixture can be made in advance, then covered and refrigerated up to 24 hours. Heat over low heat. Then stir in the sour cream and heat through.

Easy Oven Rice

12 cups boiling water
6 cups uncooked regular rice
2 tablespoons salt

Heat oven to 350°. In each of 2 ungreased baking dishes, 13½x9x2 inches, or 3-quart casseroles, mix half the boiling water, half the rice, and half the salt. Cover; cook in oven until liquid is absorbed and rice is tender, 25 to 30 minutes. Fluff with fork.

GREEN SALAD PROVENCE

1 pound spinach
2 large heads lettuce
1 can (about 15 ounces) pitted
   ripe olives, drained
4 jars (6 ounces each) marinated
   artichoke hearts
2 bottles (8 ounces each) herb
   salad dressing

Tear greens into bite-size pieces (about 24 cups). Divide greens between 2 large plastic bags; close bags and refrigerate.

Just before serving, add to each bag ½ can olives, 2 jars artichoke hearts (with liquid), and 1 bottle salad dressing. Close bags tightly and shake until greens are coated. Empty salad into large bowl.   *24 servings.*

TWIN ICE-CREAM BOMBES

4 pints orange sherbet
2 pints pistachio ice cream
2 pints chocolate ice cream

Slightly soften 2 pints of the orange sherbet; spoon one pint into each of 2 chilled 1½- to 2-quart metal molds or bowls. Freeze until firm, at least 1 hour. Slightly soften pistachio ice cream; spread 1 pint over orange sherbet in each mold. Freeze until firm. Repeat with chocolate ice cream and then with remaining orange sherbet. Cover molds with waxed paper; freeze until firm.

To unmold, turn molds onto chilled serving plates. Dip a cloth into hot water; wring out and place around top of each mold for just a few minutes. Lift off molds. Return to freezer (at this point, bombes can be wrapped in freezer wrap and stored up to 1 month); remove 15 to 30 minutes before serving. If desired, pipe with whipped cream and trim with fruit.   *24 servings (about ⅔ cup each).*

NOTE: These flavors create a vivid mold. You may prefer to substitute more-delicate pastel shades, or you may want to choose flavors keyed to your color scheme. Consider these combinations: cherry, chocolate chip, and chocolate; chocolate, French vanilla, and coffee; pistachio, dark cherry, and coffee.

A BUFFET FOR 50

Rosé Punch

Turkey and Ham Tetrazzini

Relish Trays

Tiny Hot Rolls

Ice-cream Molds or Ice-cream Balls

*Square Tiered Wedding Cake (page 58)
or Multilayer Bars*

Coffee   Tea

Here's an ideal plan for a dinner reception or engagement party. And even though it's for fifty, you can handle all of the preparation yourself (much of it can be done in advance).

Do work out a detailed system for serving and clearing. Chances are, with a party this size, you'll want to hire a few people to help out. (In many communities members of the church guild often volunteer their services for a reception held in the church hall—be sure to look into this possibility.) Run through what you want done with the people who will be helping you. Tell them exactly what you want them to do and when you want them to do it. Then make a follow-up checklist (just to be on the safe side). Write out any instructions for reheating; spell out any tray arrangements.

The meal can be served buffet style (see the diagram at right; two lines will make the service faster), and the wedding cake can double as the centerpiece. Or if you prefer, wait until the buffet table has been cleared; then bring on the cake, ice cream, and coffee.

With a crowd this size, you'll also want to give extra thought to the seating arrangement. A combination of large and small tables is lovely for an out-of-doors party; for a large room indoors, a traditional U-shaped arrangement would probably be more successful.

ROSE PUNCH

- **6 bottles (⅘ quart each) rosé, chilled**
- **1½ cups grenadine syrup, chilled**
- **1½ cups lemon juice, chilled**
- **3 quarts ginger ale, chilled**

Pour half each of the rosé, grenadine syrup, and lemon juice into 2 punch bowls; stir half the ginger ale into each bowl. Serve immediately.   *60 servings (about ½ cup each).*

NOTE: Because ginger ale becomes "flat" so quickly, it is best to prepare additional punch as it is needed (see the chart below).

SERVINGS (ABOUT ½ CUP)			
	20	80	100
Rosé	2 bottles	8 bottles	10 bottles
Grenadine Syrup	½ cup	2 cups	2½ cups
Lemon Juice	½ cup	2 cups	2½ cups
Ginger Ale	1 quart	4 quarts	5 quarts

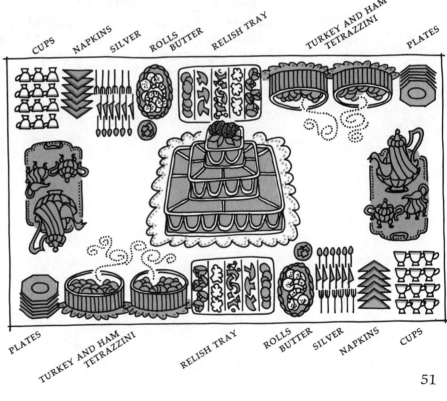

CUPS   NAPKINS   SILVER   ROLLS BUTTER   RELISH TRAY   TURKEY AND HAM TETRAZZINI   PLATES

PLATES   TURKEY AND HAM TETRAZZINI   RELISH TRAY   ROLLS BUTTER   SILVER   NAPKINS   CUPS

TURKEY AND HAM TETRAZZINI

For easier handling, prepare four casseroles at a time (the recipe is easy to divide). A willing neighbor might keep four ready-to-bake casseroles in her refrigerator and then bake them for you in time for the party. Then with four casseroles ready and waiting in your oven, you'll be fully prepared for refills.

    8 packages (7 ounces each) elbow
       spaghetti (16 cups)
  ½ cup salad oil
    8 cans (10½ ounces each) condensed
       cream of mushroom soup
    8 cans (10½ ounces each) condensed
       cream of chicken soup
 1½ quarts milk
  16 cups cubed cooked turkey* or
       chicken
    4 cups cubed cooked ham**
    2 cups chopped green pepper (about 3)
    3 cans (5¾ ounces each) pitted ripe
       olives, drained and cut into halves
       (4 cups)
    4 cups grated Parmesan cheese
    1 pound slivered almonds (4 cups)

Heat oven to 375°. In each of two 12-quart kettles, heat 8 quarts water and 3 tablespoons salt to boiling. Add half the spaghetti (8 cups) to each kettle; heat to boiling. Cook until tender, 6 to 8 minutes. Drain; pour oil over spaghetti and toss.

In each of 8 ungreased 2-quart casseroles, mix 1 can cream of mushroom soup, 1 can cream of chicken soup, and ¾ cup milk. Stir 2 cups turkey, ½ cup ham, 4 cups cooked spaghetti, ¼ cup green pepper, and ½ cup olives into each casserole. Sprinkle ½ cup Parmesan cheese over each.

Bake uncovered 30 minutes. Sprinkle ½ cup almonds on each casserole for the last 10 minutes of baking. Garnish with pimiento and parsley.   *50 servings (about 1 cup each).*

*From 6- to 6½-pound boneless turkey roast, cut into ½-inch cubes.
**From 3-pound canned ham, cut into ½-inch cubes.

NOTE: The casseroles can be prepared in advance, then covered and refrigerated up to 24 hours. Bake 40 minutes.

RELISH TRAYS

Prepare four relish trays. Place two trays on the buffet table and refrigerate the others to keep fresh looking and ready to use as refills. One round tray, 15 inches in diameter, or one rectangular tray, 18x13 inches, will hold 12 to 15 servings.

Prepare Sweet-and-Sour Relishes (below), then choose from among the following:

    Leaf, Bibb, or romaine lettuce
    2 large bunches radishes, cut into roses
    1 pint cherry tomatoes
    1 small cauliflower, separated into
       flowerets
    2 cucumbers (unpared), thinly sliced
    2 green peppers, sliced into rings or strips
    1 jar (16 ounces) pimiento-stuffed
       olives, drained
    1 jar (16 ounces) pickle chips, drained
    1 jar (8 ounces) pickled mushrooms,
       drained
    2 jars (6 ounces each) marinated
       artichoke hearts, drained

Line each tray with lettuce leaves. Place ¼ of Sweet-and-Sour Relishes in bowl in center of each round tray; if using rectangular trays, spoon a row across center width of each.

Select 5 other relishes for each round tray; arrange spoke-fashion around bowl in center. Select 4 other relishes for each rectangular tray; arrange in 2 parallel rows on each side of Sweet-and-Sour Relishes.   *4 relish trays.*

Sweet-and-Sour Relishes

    2 cups vinegar
    2 cups water
    2 cups sugar
    2 teaspoons salt
  16 stalks celery, cut into 3x¼-inch strips
    8 large carrots, cut diagonally
       into ⅛-inch slices
    3 medium onions, cut into thin slices
       and separated into rings

In large saucepan, heat vinegar, water, sugar, and salt to boiling, stirring occasionally. Place vegetables in large bowl. Pour hot mixture over vegetables; cover and refrigerate at least 4 hours. Remove to trays with slotted spoon.

TINY HOT ROLLS

    1 package active dry yeast
1½ cups warm water (105 to 115°)
    ⅔ cup sugar
1½ teaspoons salt
    ⅔ cup shortening
    2 eggs
    1 cup lukewarm mashed potatoes
    7 to 7½ cups all-purpose flour*
       Soft butter or margarine

In large mixing bowl, dissolve yeast in warm water. Stir in sugar, salt, shortening, eggs, potatoes, and 4 cups of the flour. Beat until smooth. Mix in enough remaining flour to make dough easy to handle.

Turn dough onto lightly floured board; knead until smooth and elastic, about 5 minutes. Place in greased bowl; turn greased side up. Cover tightly; refrigerate at least 8 hours. (At this point, dough can be refrigerated up to 5 days.)

Punch down dough; divide into 4 equal parts. Shape bits of dough from 1 part into thirty-six 1-inch balls. Place in lightly greased layer pan, 9x1½ inches. Brush with butter. Repeat with remaining parts of dough. (You will have 4 pans, each containing 36 balls.) Let rise 1½ hours.

Heat oven to 400°. Bake 15 to 25 minutes. *12 dozen rolls (144).*

*If using self-rising flour, omit salt.

TO FREEZE: Cool completely, wrap in aluminum foil, and freeze. (Do not freeze longer than 9 months.) To thaw, heat foil-wrapped rolls in 350° oven 25 to 30 minutes or leave at room temperature 2 to 3 hours.

BAKERY BREADS

Think about ordering small dinner rolls from a nearby bakery—cloverleafs, Parker House, croissants, or any specialty roll. Wrap in aluminum foil and heat at 350° (about 10 minutes). You can even order the rolls well in advance and freeze them. Ask the bakery for reheating recommendations.

ICE-CREAM MOLDS OR BALLS

Order individual molds from your local ice-cream store or dairy. You can choose from a wide variety of shapes and flavors (colors) to blend with your color scheme.

Be sure to get the dealer's recommendations for packing the molds for easy serving. And don't forget to ask how long before serving they should be removed from the freezer. If your freezer space is limited, the dealer might be willing to store the molds and then deliver them just in time for serving.

You can make ice-cream balls yourself. Use a large (#12) scoop and figure on 6 to 8 balls from 1 quart of ice cream. (You will need about 9 quarts to make 50 balls.) For a festive touch, roll each ball in flaked coconut (tinted if you like). Work quickly from 1 quart at a time. Place ice-cream balls on a baking sheet or piece of heavy cardboard and freeze, then cover tightly or pack in cake boxes, overwrap, and return to freezer. (Don't freeze longer than 1 month.)

CHOCOLATE-ALMOND BARS

    1 package (18.5 ounces) yellow cake
       mix with pudding
    ⅔ cup butter or margarine, softened
    ¼ cup brown sugar (packed)
    3 eggs, separated
    1 tablespoon granulated sugar
    1 package (6 ounces) semisweet
       chocolate pieces
    ⅓ cup sliced unblanched almonds

Heat oven to 350°. In large bowl, mix about half the cake mix, the butter, brown sugar and egg yolks until smooth. Stir in remaining cake mix. Press evenly in ungreased jelly roll pan, 15½x10½x1 inch. In small mixer bowl, beat egg whites until foamy. Beat in granulated sugar until soft peaks form. Spread over layer in pan; sprinkle with chocolate pieces and almonds. Bake until top is golden brown, 25 to 30 minutes. Run knife around edges while warm to loosen sides; cool. Cut into bars, 1½x1 inch.   *About 100 bars.*

When will you do what? Be sure to make out a detailed preparation schedule.

A SIMPLE RECEPTION FOR 150

Golden Glow Punch

Assorted Candies   *Salted Nuts*

Traditional Tiered Wedding Cake (page 60)

Coffee   *Tea*

Simple but elegant—these are the key words for this "I did it myself" wedding reception. It's the kind of plan that promotes the happy mingling of all the guests.

Everything can go on one table, with the wedding cake taking center stage. For faster service or greater mobility, consider placing the cake on a small honor table; then have two or three larger tables identically arrayed with the candies and nuts. And why not have the punch at one table, champagne at another, and coffee and tea at the third? Indeed, something for everyone!

You'll find a number of candy recipes here for your consideration. Select the candies that help carry out the color scheme of your flowers and other decorations. If friends want to help, let them. Farm out the candies, a batch here and a batch there. But be sure to let the helpers know exactly what colors and trims you have in mind—as well as how many candies you're counting on. Then visit your local candy stores; take a look at their selections and choose with an eye to filling out the serving plates. (Most stores will make candies to order, in the shapes and colors you like—providing you give them enough notice.) If you prefer, you can even buy all the candies for your reception. What could be easier?

Be sure to consult the Quantity Shopping Guide on page 56 for additional help. There you will find how-much-is-enough guidelines for buying coffee, tea, cream, sugar, candy, nuts, and your other menu needs.

GOLDEN GLOW PUNCH

- **6** cans (6 ounces each) frozen orange juice concentrate (thawed)
- **6** cans (6 ounces each) frozen lemonade concentrate (thawed)
- **6** quarts apple juice, chilled
- **12** quarts ginger ale, chilled
- **3** quarts lemon or orange sherbet, if desired
- **Ice Rings (page 49), if desired**

Pour half the concentrate and half the apple juice into each of 2 large punch bowls; stir half the ginger ale into each bowl. Spoon in sherbet (try lemon sherbet in one bowl, orange in the other) or add an Ice Ring. Serve immediately. *150 servings (about ½ cup each).*

NOTE: Be ready for refills. Prepare additional punch as you need it according to the chart below.

SERVINGS (ABOUT ½ CUP)

	25	50	75	100
Orange Juice	1 can	2 cans	3 cans	4 cans
Lemonade	1 can	2 cans	3 cans	4 cans
Apple Juice	1 quart	2 quarts	3 quarts	4 quarts
Ginger Ale	2 quarts	4 quarts	6 quarts	8 quarts
Sherbet	1 pint	2 pints	3 pints	4 pints

SPICY SUGARED NUTS

- **2** egg whites
- **8** cups pecans or walnut halves
- **1** cup sugar
- **¼** cup cinnamon

Heat oven to 300°. Mix egg whites and nuts in large bowl. Stir until nuts are coated and sticky. Mix sugar and cinnamon; sprinkle over nuts. Stir until sugar mixture completely coats nuts. Spread on 2 ungreased baking sheets. Bake 30 minutes.   *About 8 cups.*

NOTE: This recipe will serve about 60 people. You can extend the quantity by adding 2 or 3 pounds of assorted nuts. Or why not repeat this recipe a few times? It's easy to handle in the amounts specified.

APRICOT-NUT BALLS

1 package (8 ounces) dried apricots, ground or finely cut up
2½ cups flaked coconut
⅔ cup finely chopped nuts
¾ cup sweetened condensed milk
　Confectioners' sugar

Mix apricots, coconut, nuts, and milk. Shape mixture into 1-inch balls; roll in confectioners' sugar. Let candies stand until firm, about 2 hours.　*48 candies.*

PASTEL WAFERS

3 tablespoons butter or margarine
2 tablespoons milk
1 package (15.4 ounces) creamy white frosting mix
½ to 1 teaspoon flavoring, if desired
　Few drops food color

Heat butter in milk in 2-quart saucepan over medium heat until butter melts. Remove from heat; stir in frosting mix (dry). Continue stirring with rubber scraper until smooth, about 2 minutes. Stir in flavoring and food color.

Drop mixture by teaspoonfuls onto waxed paper. Let stand until firm.　*About 6 dozen candies.*

MARZIPAN FRUITS

A choice of colorful "fruits" to fill in your candy trays. (P.S. Think about using clusters of them to decorate your cake.)

1 package (15.4 ounces) creamy white frosting mix
3 tablespoons flour
¼ cup plus 1 tablespoon butter or margarine, softened
2 tablespoons hot water
½ teaspoon almond extract
　Food color

Mix frosting mix (dry), flour, and butter with fork. Add water; work until mixture forms a ball. Knead 20 to 30 times on board lightly dusted with confectioners' sugar.

Divide fondant into 4 equal parts. Knead in your choice of food color, 1 drop at a time, for equal distribution (see suggestions below). Shape candy fruits as directed (for most fruits, use 1 teaspoonful fondant). Let stand on waxed paper until firm, then paint. Store in plastic wrap.　*4 to 5 dozen candies.*

With Yellow Fondant
Bananas: Shape fondant into rolls, then taper and curve. Paint on characteristic markings with green food color.
Pears: Make pear shapes; use stick cinnamon for each stem. Brush on diluted red food color for blush.
Peaches: Shape into small balls; make crease on each with wooden pick. Use clove for stem. Brush on diluted red food color for blush.

With Red Fondant
Apples: Shape into balls; use stick cinnamon for each stem, clove for blossom end. Brush on diluted red food color.
Strawberries: Make little heart shapes; roll in red sugar. Use a piece of green wooden pick for each stem.

With Orange Fondant
Oranges: Shape into balls; roll in orange sugar. Use clove for each blossom end.
Apricots: Shape into small balls; make crease on each with wooden pick. Use clove for stem. Brush on diluted red food color.
Pumpkins: Roll into balls; make several creases on sides and flatten each top slightly. Use green wooden pick for stem end. Brush with diluted red and yellow food color.

With Green Fondant
Green Apples: Shape into balls; use stick cinnamon for each stem, clove for blossom end. Brush on diluted red food color.

MOLDED FONDANT FLOWERS

Prepare fondant for Marzipan Fruits (left) and tint as desired. Shape into 1-inch balls; dip into sugar. Press into small plastic flower and leaf molds; unmold at once. Let stand on waxed paper until firm.　*About 100 candies.*

apricot
banana
peach
strawberry
pear
apple
pumpkin

CANDY RIBBONS

    2 tablespoons butter or margarine
    ¼ cup milk
    1 package (15.4 ounces) creamy white
      frosting mix
    2 tablespoons butter or margarine
    ¼ cup milk
    1 package (14.3 ounces) lemon
      frosting mix

Line bottom of square pan, 8x8x2 inches, with aluminum foil, leaving 1 inch of foil at opposite sides. In medium saucepan, heat 2 tablespoons butter and ¼ cup milk over low heat until butter melts and mixture *just* begins to simmer. Remove from heat; stir in white frosting mix (dry). Heat over low heat, stirring constantly with rubber scraper, until smooth and glossy, 1 to 2 minutes. *Do not overcook.* Spread mixture evenly in pan.

   Repeat with remaining 2 tablespoons butter, ¼ cup milk, and the lemon frosting mix. Spread lemon mixture evenly over white mixture. Chill until firm. Lift candy out; cut into pieces, 1x¼ inch.   *About 200 candies.*

CANDIED ORANGE PEEL

With sharp knife, score peel of 2 large oranges into quarters; remove peel gently. Heat orange peel and 6 cups water to boiling. Simmer 30 minutes; drain. Repeat process, cooking peel in another 6 cups water. With spoon, gently scrape off remaining white membrane from peel. Cut peel lengthwise into ¼-inch strips.

   Heat 2 cups sugar and 1 cup water to boiling; stir until sugar is dissolved. Add peel; simmer, stirring frequently, 45 minutes. Turn mixture into strainer; drain thoroughly. Roll peel in 1½ cups sugar; spread on waxed paper to dry.   *About ½ pound.*

INSTANT TEA CONCENTRATE

Measure 1 cup (2 ounces) instant tea into large stainless steel or glass container; stir in 2½ quarts boiling water. Mix 1 part concentrate to 2 parts boiling water to serve as needed. *Enough concentrate for 45 servings (about ⅔ cup each).*

QUANTITY SHOPPING GUIDE

Tea	1 pound = 6 cups loose tea = about 200 servings (1 cup each)
Coffee	1 pound = 5 cups ground = 40 to 50 servings (1 cup each)
	1 jar instant (6 ounces) = 90 to 100 servings (1 cup each)
Cream	1 pint = 32 servings (1 tablespoon each)
Sugar	1 pound = 2 cups or 90 large or 110 small cubes
Lemon	5 large lemons = 50 thin slices
Champagne	1 bottle (4/5 quart) = 8 glasses (3 ounces each)
Punch	1 gallon = about 30 servings (½ cup each)
Turkey	6- to 6½-pound boneless roast = 16 cups (½-inch cubes)
Ham	3-pound (canned) = 4 cups (½-inch cubes)
French Bread	1 loaf (1 pound) = 24 to 28 slices (½ inch thick)
Butter	1 pound = 48 squares (2 teaspoons each)
Ice Cream	1 quart = 8 servings or balls (#12 scoop)
Candy	1 pound (small candies) = 50 servings
Nuts	
Almonds (shelled)	1 pound = 3½ cups
Mixed, salted	1 pound = 30 servings
Pecans (shelled)	1 pound = 4 cups
Walnuts (shelled)	1 pound = 4 cups
Relishes	
Celery	1 bunch (12 stalks) = 25 servings
Radishes	6 to 8 bunches = 25 servings
Carrots (raw)	3 to 4 large, cut into 3-inch strips = 25 servings
Pickles	1 quart (sliced) = 25 servings (about 2 each)
Olives	1 quart = 25 servings (about 2 each)

WEDDING CAKES

Large or small, formal or informal, every wedding calls for a wedding cake. And what better way to have just the kind of cake you want than to make it yourself! (Or ask a friend with a talent for baking and decorating to make the cake as her wedding gift to you.) Look over the following recipes carefully. Chances are one of these cakes will be perfect for your plans. And even if you're having a catered reception or buying your cake from a bakery, you're bound to pick up an idea or two.

Remember, no one ever said a wedding cake *must* be a white cake with white icing. Try a chocolate cake with white icing and chocolate decorations. Or a white icing with yellow, green, or rose accents. Or go with an overall tinted icing with deeper hued trims. Don't be afraid to match cake colors with your flowers and other decorations.

Stick to basic flavors for the cake itself—icing colors can be weakened or strengthened. But you're stuck with the finished layers.

If you have something very special in mind for your wedding cake, make sure the person or bakery making the cake is right on your wavelength. Your idea of pale peach may be several shades lighter than someone else's. When it comes to color, you can't do too much checking.

Have you ever encountered charms in a wedding cake? It's a charming old custom that makes a delightful lottery of cutting the cake. Tiny coins, rings, thimbles, and the like are individually wrapped in foil and baked throughout the various tiers of the cake. Supposedly, they "tell the fortune" of the person who happens to get a particular charm in his slice of cake. (Any baker will have these available or can tell you where to get them.)

TWIN HEARTS WEDDING CAKE

Special heart-shaped pans make this romantic cake—nice for a small reception or prewedding party.

YOU WILL NEED:

2 packages (18.5 ounces each) white cake mix with pudding
2 packages (7.2 ounces each) fluffy white frosting mix

Heat oven to 350°. Grease and flour 2 heart-shaped layer pans, 9 inches at the widest part and 1½ inches deep. Prepare cake mix, 1 package at a time, as directed. Bake in heart-shaped pans until top springs back when touched lightly in center, 30 to 35 minutes. Cool.

Prepare frosting mix, 1 package at a time, as directed. Tint frosting if desired. (You might even want to give some thought to using a different color on each cake.)

Place cakes on a large tray or mirror or on 2 smaller ones. Fill each 2 layers with frosting. Frost sides and tops of cakes, swirling frosting for a decorative effect. (For additional decorating tips and ideas, see pages 62-63.)

Cut each cake into 15 pieces as shown in the diagram. *25 to 30 servings.*

NOTE: For a larger party, make this recipe twice—place a Twin Hearts Cake at each end of the table.

SQUARE TIERED WEDDING CAKE

Three square tiers form an unusual but very attractive shape for this cake for 50 to 60 guests. And the top layer is a fruitcake that can be saved for the first-anniversary celebration. Rely on mixes or start from "scratch"—we offer you two ways to go.

YOU WILL NEED:

**Easy Fruitcake or Jeweled Fruitcake
Easy Pound Cake or Silver White Cake
Apricot Filling
Almond extract**

6 cans (16.5 ounces each) vanilla frosting

Bake fruitcake. Then bake pound cake or Silver White Cake.

When ready to assemble cake, prepare Apricot Filling: Heat 1 jar (12 ounces) apricot jam and 1 tablespoon water to boiling, stirring occasionally. Strain and cool.

To assemble cake, place one 13x9x2-inch layer top side down on 18-inch square tray, mirror, or serving plate. Cut second 13x9x2-inch layer lengthwise in half, making two 13x 4½x2-inch layers (see diagram 1). Place one half top side down against long side of layer on tray (see diagram 2).

Stir ½ teaspoon almond extract into 1 can frosting. Join parts of cake on tray with frosting and frost top. Spread ½ cup Apricot Filling thinly on frosting. Place remaining 13x9x2-inch layer and 13x4½x2-inch layer top sides up on filling (see diagram 3). Stir ½ teaspoon almond extract into each of 2 cans frosting. Frost sides and top of cake on tray.

Place one 8-inch layer top side down on foil-covered 7-inch cardboard square. Stir ½ teaspoon almond extract into 1 can frosting. Frost top of layer on cardboard. Spread remaining Apricot Filling thinly on frosting. Place remaining 8-inch layer on filling. Frost sides and top of cake. Place frosted cake (with cardboard base) on center of cake on tray.

Cut fruitcake crosswise in half, making 2 halves, 5x4½ inches. Place one half fruitcake top side up on foil-covered 4-inch cardboard square. Stir ½ teaspoon almond extract into 1 can frosting. Frost sides and top of fruitcake half. (Reserve remaining fruitcake half for another use—see page 60.) Place frosted fruitcake (with cardboard base) on center of 8-inch cake (see diagram 4).

Make fancy swirls on sides and top of cake with remaining frosting. (For additional decorating tips and ideas, see pages 62-63.)

Cut cake as directed below.   *About 70 servings (2x1½ inches each).*

To cut cake:
Remove top tier of fruitcake with cardboard; freeze and use to celebrate your first wedding anniversary.
Middle tier—Make 6 lengthwise cuts and 4 crosswise cuts (24 servings). Remove cardboard.
Bottom tier—Make 8 lengthwise cuts and 4 crosswise cuts (48 servings).

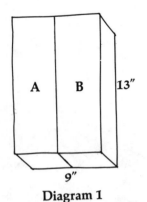

Diagram 1

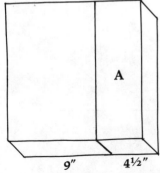

Diagram 2

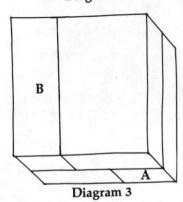

Diagram 3

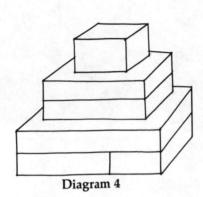

Diagram 4

EASY FRUITCAKE

1 package (14 ounces) date bar mix
²/₃ cup hot water
3 eggs
¼ cup all-purpose flour
¾ teaspoon baking powder
1 teaspoon cinnamon
¼ teaspoon nutmeg
¼ teaspoon allspice
2 tablespoons molasses
1 cup chopped nuts
1 package (8 ounces) candied whole
  red or green cherries (1 cup)
1 cup raisins

Heat oven to 325°. Grease and flour loaf pan, 9x5x3 inches. Mix date filling from date bar mix and hot water. Blend in crumbly mix, eggs, flour, baking powder, spices, and molasses. Stir in nuts and fruit. Pour into pan. Bake until wooden pick inserted in center comes out clean, about 1 hour 20 minutes. Cool.

JEWELED FRUITCAKE

1 package (8 ounces) dried apricots
  (about 2 cups)
1 package (8 ounces) pitted dates
  (about 1½ cups)
¾ pound whole Brazil nuts (1½ cups)
1 cup drained red and green
  maraschino cherries
⅓ pound red and green candied
  pineapple, cut up (about 1 cup)
¾ cup all-purpose flour*
¾ cup sugar
½ teaspoon baking powder
½ teaspoon salt
3 eggs
1½ teaspoons vanilla

Heat oven to 300°. Line loaf pan, 9x5x3 inches, with aluminum foil; grease foil. Mix all ingredients thoroughly. Spread evenly in pan.

Bake until wooden pick inserted in center comes out clean, about 1 hour 45 minutes. If necessary, cover cake with aluminum foil the last 30 minutes of baking to prevent excessive browning. Remove cake from pan; cool.

*If using self-rising flour, omit baking powder and salt.

EASY POUND CAKE

4 packages (16 ounces each) pound
  cake mix
4 teaspoons almond extract

Heat oven to 325°. Grease and flour oblong pan, 13x9x2 inches. Prepare 1 package pound cake mix as directed except—add 1 teaspoon almond extract before blending ingredients. Bake in oblong pan until top springs back when touched lightly in center, 25 to 30 minutes. Cool 10 minutes; remove from pan and cool top side up on wire rack. Repeat for second and third packages cake mix.

Grease and flour 2 square pans, 8x8x2 inches. Prepare remaining package pound cake mix as directed except—add 1 teaspoon almond extract before blending ingredients. Divide batter between square pans. Bake until top springs back when touched lightly in center, 30 to 35 minutes. Cool 10 minutes; remove from pans and cool top sides up on wire racks.

SILVER WHITE CAKE

Prepare the recipe 3 times in 13x9x2-inch pan and once in two 8x8x2-inch pans.

2¼ cups cake flour or 2 cups
  all-purpose flour*
1½ cups sugar
3½ teaspoons baking powder
1 teaspoon salt
½ cup shortening
1 cup milk
1 teaspoon vanilla
4 egg whites

Heat oven to 350°. Grease and flour oblong pan, 13x9x2 inches, or 2 square pans, 8x8x2 inches. Measure flour, sugar, baking powder, salt, shortening, ²/₃ cup of the milk, and the vanilla into large mixer bowl.

Blend on low speed ½ minute, scraping bowl constantly. Beat on high speed 2 minutes, scraping bowl occasionally. Add remaining milk and the egg whites; beat on high speed 2 minutes, scraping bowl occasionally. Pour into pan(s). Bake until wooden pick inserted in center comes out clean, oblong 35 to 40 minutes, square pans 30 to 35 minutes. Cool.

*Do not use self-rising flour in this recipe.

TRADITIONAL TIERED WEDDING CAKE

A classic three-tiered cake that will serve 150. Made easily with cake and frosting mixes—and no special pans. Assemble cake the day before the wedding.

YOU WILL NEED:

7 packages (18.5 ounces each) white cake mix with pudding

6 packages (15.4 ounces each) creamy white frosting mix

If you plan to frost and decorate the cake elaborately, have extra frosting mix ready. Prepare one or two packages at a time.

Bake cake mix, 1 package at a time, in oblong pan, 13x9x2 inches, as directed except—increase egg whites to 4. Cool.

Before assembling cake, prepare frosting mix as directed, 2 packages at a time, as needed.

To assemble cake, place 2 layers together side by side, with top sides down, on 22x18-inch tray or mirror. Frost top. Place another 2 layers together, with top sides down, on frosted layers. Frost sides and top.

Place 1 layer top side down on foil-covered 11½x7½-inch cardboard. (The cake should overlap the cardboard evenly on all sides.) Frost top. Place another layer top side down on the frosted layer on cardboard. Frost sides and top. Place frosted cake (with cardboard base) on center of first tier with long sides parallel.

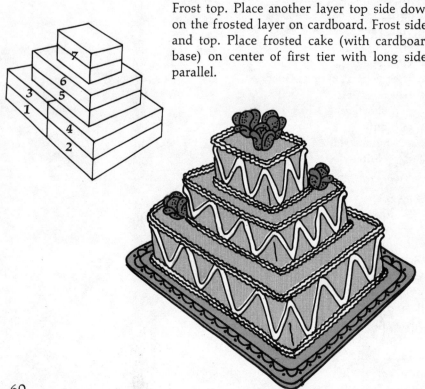

Cut remaining layer crosswise in half. Place one half top side down on foil-covered 7½ x 5½-inch cardboard. (The cake should overlap the cardboard evenly on all sides.) Frost top. Place other half top side down on the frosted layer on cardboard. Frost sides and top. Place frosted cake (with cardboard base) on center of second tier with long sides parallel.

Make fancy swirls on sides and top of cake. (For additional decorating tips and ideas, see pages 62-63.) Cover with plastic wrap until ready to serve. Cut cake as directed below. *About 160 servings (2x1 inch each).*

To cut cake:

Top tier—Make 4 lengthwise cuts and 6 crosswise cuts (24 servings). Remove cardboard.

Middle tier—Make 4 lengthwise cuts and 12 crosswise cuts (48 servings). Remove cardboard.

Bottom tier—Make 4 lengthwise cuts and 24 crosswise cuts (96 servings).

THE GROOM'S CAKE

The "groom's cake," traditionally a fruitcake, is often frosted as the top tier of the wedding cake (see the Square Tiered Wedding Cake). The lower tiers of the cake are cut and served to the guests; the very special top tier is carefully wrapped and frozen—for the first anniversary.

The "groom's cake" may also be a separate cake, cut into 1-inch pieces and individually wrapped in tiny white boxes or aluminum foil and trimmed with ribbon or artificial flowers. The tiny packages are then arranged on trays at the reception, and each guest takes one home to "dream on." You can make these yourself, in a limited quantity. Simply prepare the batter for Easy Fruitcake or Jeweled Fruitcake and spoon about 1 tablespoon into nut cups or miniature paper baking cups (on baking sheet). Bake in 325° oven 25 minutes. (Makes about 3½ dozen individual cakes.)

PETITS FOURS WEDDING CAKE

The easiest tiered cake of all—simply arrange Petits Fours on a tiered plate. No cutting problems at all. For a larger crowd, you can make this recipe several times. Or order Petits Fours from the bakery—and choose frostings that will complement your color scheme.

YOU WILL NEED:

1 package (18.5 ounces) white cake mix
with pudding
Apricot Glaze (below)
Petits Fours Icing (below)
Decorators' Icing (right), if desired

Bake cake mix in jelly roll pan, 15½x10½x1 inch, as directed. Cool cake in pan. Cut cake into small squares, diamonds, and triangles

To glaze cake pieces, secure each piece with fork, hold over saucepan, and pour warm Apricot Glaze over each. Place on wire rack; let stand about 1 hour or until set.

Coat glazed cake pieces with Petits Fours Icing by placing upside down, a few at a time, on wire rack over large bowl or baking dish. Pour icing over top so entire cake piece is covered at one time. (Icing that drips off the cake pieces and into the bowl can be reheated and used again.)

Decorate tops with simple flower designs made with Decorators' Icing, tiny candy flowers, or silver dragées. (For additional decorating tips and ideas, see pages 62-63.) Arrange cake pieces on a tiered plate.

If you wish, choose a simple decoration (fresh or artificial flowers, paper bells, a pretty bow) for the center of the top tier. *About 35 servings (2x2 inches each).*

Apricot Glaze: Heat 1 jar (12 ounces) apricot preserves and 3 tablespoons water; strain.

Petits Fours Icing: In top of double boiler, mix 9 cups sifted confectioners' sugar (about 2 pounds), ½ cup water, ½ cup light corn syrup, 1 teaspoon vanilla, and ½ teaspoon almond extract until smooth. Heat over boiling water just to lukewarm. (Do not overheat icing or it will become dull.) Remove from heat, leaving icing over hot water to keep it thin. If you like, tint portions of icing with your choice of food colors. If necessary, stir in a few drops of hot water until proper consistency.

Decorators' Icing: Mix 2 cups confectioners' sugar and 1 tablespoon water until smooth. Stir in additional water, 1 teaspoon at a time, until icing is of the consistency that can be used easily in a decorators' tube and yet hold its shape. Tint with food color if desired. *¾ cup.*

NOTE: Silver White Cake (page 59) can be substituted for the white cake mix. Bake cake as directed except—pour batter into greased and floured jelly roll pan, 15½x10½x1 inch. Bake 25 minutes. Cool in pan.

NOTE: If your own tiered server is too small to hold all the Petits Fours attractively, be sure to check the stock in your local department and variety stores before giving up the idea. Tiered cake plates are now readily available in a variety of shapes and sizes—clear or colored, in plastic, metal, milk glass, and even crystal. Separate decorative tier supports can also be purchased to use with your own cake plates or (good idea!) custom-cut and sprayed wooden trays. With these, you can create any effect you wish. And for a large crowd, consider using two tiered servers.

TIPS ON BAKING AND FREEZING

Cakes can be baked 1 or 2 days before the wedding. Cool cakes completely. Do not frost. Wrap in plastic wrap or aluminum foil and store at room temperature or in the refrigerator.

To assure ease in removing cakes from pans, grease and flour pans *thoroughly* as directed on the package or in the recipe.

Cakes can also be baked at your convenience a few layers at a time up to 2 months in advance of the wedding day. Cool cakes completely. Do not frost. Freeze uncovered 2 hours, then remove from freezer. Wrap in freezer wrap and, if you wish, pack in boxes. Return to freezer.

Thaw frozen cakes in wrapper at room temperature 45 minutes. Then remove wrapper carefully and thaw uncovered cakes at room temperature 1 hour.

TIPS ON FROSTING

Cool cakes completely on wire racks before frosting; brush off all loose crumbs. Frost cake first with a *very thin* layer of frosting to seal in any excess crumbs, then frost more lavishly for a decorative effect. A small flexible spatula is best for frosting.

Always frost the side of the cake first, using an upward stroke and building up a little ridge of frosting above the top of the cake. Then frost the top, spreading the frosting to meet the ridge.

You can frost your cake right on the serving plate if you begin by placing several strips of waxed paper on the serving plate, then place the unfrosted cake on the strips. When you are finished frosting and decorating the cake, pull out the strips—you'll have a clean plate.

Cakes frosted with creamy-type frosting can be stored covered overnight. To keep the wrapping from touching the frosting or upsetting the decorations, insert several wooden picks into the top and around the edges of the cake (let the picks stick up quite a bit). Then form a loose tent of aluminum foil or plastic wrap over the cake.

Cakes frosted with fluffy-type frostings are best when served the same day they are frosted.

TIPS ON DECORATING

The first rule of decorating: Don't overdo. Think of your cake as a dress and your decorations as the accessories. They must work together to be successful.

You can decorate without a decorators' tube: Use a flexible spatula to create a draping effect, straight up-and-down columns, elegant swirls, or overlapping scallops. (See sketches below.)

If you're going to use a decorators' tube, plan your designs on paper first. Will you decorate the sides and top? Or simply pipe around the edges? (See page 63.)

If your cake is tiered, use a decorators' tube to fill in any gaps at the base of each tier. (The petal tip is pretty for this.)

To add a touch of color, try an icing blossom here and there or add a sparkle of glamour with silver dragées. Or use a few clusters of Gumdrop Roses or Gumdrop Flowers (both on page 63). Marzipan Fruits (page 55) are also pretty. The flowers and fruits would also be nice around the base of the cake.

If your frosting is white, go traditional with white trims...or decorate with a touch of color. If you've chosen a tinted frosting, maybe your decorations should be a slightly darker hue.

Do you plan to "theme" your decorations? Think about the zodiac, nature's colors, spring flowers, or anything that has a special meaning for you.

For the top of the cake, use flowers (fresh, artificial, or icing) or bows. Or you can purchase bride and groom figures or bells.

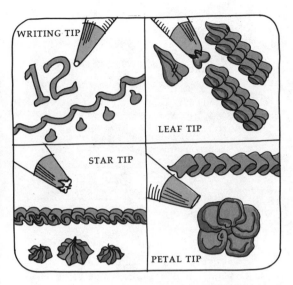

WRITING TIP

LEAF TIP

STAR TIP

PETAL TIP

USING A DECORATORS' TUBE

If there are no special instructions from the manufacturer, it is generally best to hold the tube at a 45° angle. Hold it securely with one hand near the top of the tube; use the other hand to guide the tip.

One exception: For rosettes and other "drop" flowers, it's best to hold the tube straight up and down.

Always try a few practice strokes or flowers on waxed paper before decorating the cake itself.

Here are a few of the most common and versatile tips:

Writing tip—For delicate outlines, lattice work, narrow borders, numbers, letters.
Leaf tip—For leaves, of course, but also for long, delicate petals, elaborate borders.
Star tip—For small, frilly borders, simple "drop" flowers, rosettes.
Petal tip—For petals, ribbons, flowing borders.

Use the following icing in your decorators' tube. The consistency can be varied so that it will be stiff enough to work with easily.

Creamy Decorators' Frosting: Prepare 1 package (15.4 ounces) creamy white frosting mix as directed except—mix in confectioners sugar, about 1 tablespoon at a time, until frosting is stiff enough to hold its shape yet be used easily in the decorators' tube.

GUMDROP FLOWERS

Make these pretty flowers with 1 package (15.4 ounces) creamy white frosting mix. Prepare the frosting as directed and tint as desired. (Try different colors or two shades of the same color.)

For each flower, put a medium-size gumdrop on a wooden pick. Fill the tip end of a teaspoon with frosting; level off along edge of bowl. Draw spoon down over gumdrop, making a petal. (Frosting must be stiff.)

Turn the gumdrop and continue adding petals—2 or 3 rows, depending on size of gumdrop and shape of spoon (½ cup makes 5 or 6 flowers). Arrange clusters of 3 or 4 flowers on each tier. Nice for the top of the cake too.

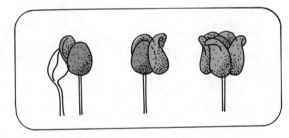

GUMDROP ROSES

Choose gumdrops in a variety of colors or all the same color.

For each rose, roll 4 large gumdrops on well-sugared board into ⅛-inch-thick ovals. Sprinkle sugar on ovals; cut each in half. Roll one half-oval tightly to form the center of rose. Place more half-ovals around center, overlapping slightly, and press together at base. Trim base. Cut leaves from rolled green gumdrops. Arrange as desired on cake.

SUBJECT INDEX

RECIPE INDEX